How Healthy is Your Church?

Dr. Alton E. Loveless

All scripture verses are from the
KJV, or other translations noted
This book was printed in the United States of America.

To order additional copies of this book contact:

FWB Publications
Enchanted Acres
1006 Rayme Drive
Columbus, Ohio 43207
Alton.loveless@prodigy.net
Dr. Alton Loveless, Owner

FWB

Dedicated

To

Mom Lane

My

Junior Sunday school Teacher

Who Led Me To Know Jesus.

Thanks Mrs. Ollie Lane

For The Last

65 Years Of Blessedness

Table of Contents

Preface

TO A SUNDAY SCHOOL TEACHER
By Cecil Teachout

Don't say a child's too little when he's five or six or seven;
Don't neglect to ask him if he's sure he'll go to heaven.

Don't wait until a week from now to make salvation plain;
That little one within your reach may not be there again.

Remember that our Father sees the end from the beginning;
And these little ones so precious should be saved from lives of sinning.

We must bring each one to Jesus. They must meet Him face to face;
They must take him as their Savior, they must know his matchless grace.

He is knocking at their heart's door now, as you give to them God's Word;
He is seeking to gain entrance, so that He may be their Lord.

If one of those, whom you have taught, is never saved--but lost,
And spends eternity in hell-- How can we count the cost?

God caused that little one to come so we could point the way,
And lead him to accept the Christ, so he'd be saved today.

Introduction
Where it all began

There were no surprises from the poll sent to nearly 2000 pastors and church workers. The following responses festered within me until I wanted to attempt to do what one of my friends said in his reply to my personal letter to him.

This book is a compilation of the responses I received and an attempt to gather the storehouse of material that I have on my computer obtained over the years. I have been mentored by such men as Dr. Stan Toler, Dr. John Maxwell, Dr. Gary McIntosh, Charles Arn, Win Arn, Dr. Thom Rainer, Dr. Elmer towns, Lyle Schaller, Dr. Kenneth Gangel, Dr. Lawrence Richards and noted pollsters George Barna, George Gallup and David Kinnaman. I hope I have given credit property to those that I have included and regret that I did not know the sources of all my material. Much of my material came from individuals and denominations which I felt would be beneficial in improving the Sunday school and church life. Likewise some of the material may appear repetitious at times but was necessary to include at that point to give credence to the subject at hand. Most of material has no need for explanations so you can draw your conclusions and make it applicable to your situation whether your church is small or large, country, urban or city.

The story begins:

Good morning Alton,
I received your letter asking for help about the Sunday school. I trust you'll be able to write a good book, especially for the Free Will Baptists. I pray that your book will point out the problems Sunday school has now, and why it is in decline. Also, you need to point out a path to renewal.

The part of your book that points out the decline, can be well documented. However, the second part of your book that talks about renewal will be more difficult to document. I would think that the best way to document your book is to find Free Will Baptist churches that are growing today in spite of the decline around them.

Elmer L. Towns, Co-*Founder, Liberty University*

Following are the questions in the e-mail send from my personal and company lists.

1. If you are a Sunday school Superintendent, what is your biggest need?

2. If you are a Sunday school teacher what areas do you think you need help in?

3. Do you feel the Sunday school is doing a good job in training you to fulfill the task given you?

4. Does your church have training for its staff of teachers? Who teaches the classes? What material do you use for the teaching?

5. If I were writing a book on Sunday school this is what I would write about.

6. My Sunday school is not growing because of.....

7. My Sunday school is growing because of.

8. My Sunday school has an outreach growth approach

9. My Sunday school is organized for each age group

10. Our superintendent has a regular time to teach the teachers how to teach their children.

11. Our encouragement usually comes from

12. Our pastor does or does not promote the Sunday school.

13. Counting the amount of people in your worship service, what percentage of them come to Sunday school?

14. If I were a Sunday school superintendent I would introduce this to the Sunday school program.

⟋⟍

The first question I asked on the poll that I had sent to just short of 2000 Sunday school workers and pastors was, *"If you are a Sunday school Superintendent what is your biggest need?"* To my amazement only one out of all the respondents actually had a superintendent. The majority of those who made an attempt to answer this question said we cannot keep a superintendent or find someone who actually does the job.

"If you are a Sunday school teacher what areas do you think you need help in?" was the second question I asked. Responses such as:

- I have great needs for a helper,
- I need a better classroom set-up away from the common area,
- Curriculum that would help me teach a class with more than a range of three years in the students age,
- The need for a prayer chairman, outreach coordinator and a care chairman to contact missing members and coordinate follow-up with our guest and absentees.
- One of the more common responses was the need for curriculum that connects the text to the student's grade level while applying it to the student's daily lives in meaningful ways.
- Some the responses for the older age classes were:
- How to better understand the postmodern mindset,
- How to communicate to others the importance of Sunday school,
- The need for backup teachers when one is out of town are on vacation,
- To have different classes for singles versus the traditional married folk who have kids or blended families. His

comment what type single will reflect issues radically different than blended families and those who are different than traditionally married people with children.

- A publisher said, "I often grieve over churches that have lost the concept and wisdom of scope and sequence has curriculum presented, rather than picking and choosing each Sunday what they wanted to teach."
- A Sunday school attendee suggested that there be curriculum that would address aging needs, dealing with the death of a spouse, illness, grief, heaven, discouragement, and staying active in the service regardless of age. He further remarked that for young leadership it is important to recognize the value of the seniors and engage them into the big scheme of the church and Sunday school and not be disinterested in their activities.

3. *Do you feel the Sunday school is doing a good job in training you to fulfill the task given you?* In all the responses I received, not one church had a regular training program for their teachers. Only two said that they had a course at least once per year and that one had just started to teach their teachers recently how to teach.

4. *Does your church have training for its staff of teachers? Who teaches the classes? What material do you use for the teaching?* Of the three responses that said they had a training class, ever so little, that the trainer used his own material and only one had used The Evangelical Training Association material.

5. *If I were writing a book on Sunday school this is what I would write about.* The answers to this question was a mix bag with most being non-related to the question. Namely;

- Can it be resurrected?
- Will something else replace it?

The most likely to have won my vote responded this way:

- I would write a book on how to promote Sunday school so that the regular congregation and guests understand its importance.
- I would write on how to motivate people to join a Sunday school class.

A woman teacher said, Sunday school is the backbone of the local church.

- Teachers must be knowledgeable about the whole Bible and have the freedom to adjust materials for our needs.

- Church leadership must promote and participate in the Sunday school in order for to be successful teachers must ensure that they are being spiritually fed.

Another responded which appeared to be coming from his lack of interest when he said," I really doubt that I would write a book about Sunday school."

6. *My Sunday school is not growing because of.....* Nearly to a person the response was that it was not and to put it as one did: "Definitely not!"

7. *My Sunday school is growing because of.* Hardly any churches responded with we are growing in Sunday school, electives, or other types of Bible study. Many blamed it on the demographics of where they were located and the lack of interest in Sunday school and church. This was more common among country churches than in the city communities, however that was a similar problem among them as well. In reading all the responses I found apathy existent in nearly every returned poll.

8. *My Sunday school has an outreach growth approach.* The poll showed that there was absolutely not one church with an organized outreach program but depended only on the word-of-mouth invitations of its membership.

9. *My Sunday school is organized for each age group.* Nearly all churches were divided in an age appropriateness suggested by the publisher that they used. However some of the churches had as few as two classes, one for the children and the other for adults. Then upwards to the larger church that was closely graded throughout each of the age groups and from 5 to 6 adult classes due to the age differences or needs for electives and Bible studies of church needs. Namely, New Membership, New Convert and Bible Doctrine classes.

10. *Our Superintendent has a regular time to teach the teachers how to teach their children.* Since only one church had a superintendent there were no suggestions or responses to this question.

11. *Our encouragement usually comes from.* Since there were no training sessions by a superintendent, Director of Christian Education or pastor, the most common response to this question was the encouragement came from their own self-study and the successes they felt from teaching their class members.

12. *Our pastor does or does not promote the Sunday school.* As I recall all but one said that their pastor did recommend Sunday school with the one exception saying that even the pastor and his wife did not attend Sunday school themselves. Many of those who said the pastor did recommend Sunday school but did not suggest the importance of it as much as he did other ministries of the church.

13. *Counting the amount of people in your worship service, what percentage of them come to Sunday school.* The responses to this question were in the range of 75% all the way down to 30% of those that attended Sunday school versus those who attended church. Many said that that more people are attending church today than Sunday school which was the reverse of what had happened when they were in their youth when Sunday school exceeded the worship service in attendance.

14. *If I was a Sunday school Superintendent I would introduce this to the Sunday school program.* A pastor responded to this question by stating," there are number of additions that could be made to the program ideally.
The big three being:

- One. Outreach program;
- Two. Follow-up program;
- Three. Teacher training.

I said ideally, because it is like pulling teeth or mining diamonds to get people to have the minimal Sunday school program that we do have.

A teacher from an adult class in a city church said, we need to have multiple adult classes for each of the needs that are represented in their age group. Namely, singles, college-age, young married, senior men, senior women, married couples, grief, divorced etc.

An elementary Sunday school teacher suggested, a monthly Bible memorization program or contest for all children classes.

There were many unsolicited remarks which I am including here.

A Georgia pastor asked:
I would like to ask you a few questions.

1. Can you name any churches that have a vibrant SS ministry at the present time?

2. Can you name any churches that have had a growing SS ministry over the last decade?

3. Do you foresee other ministries replacing SS as we know it today?

4. Do we have anybody at Randall House Publication that is currently involved in a growing and thriving SS?

5. We currently have twice as many children and teens on Wednesday night than we have in Sunday school. Is that a trend you have notice in other churches?

6. We have a vibrant and growing Sunday morning worship service and Wednesday night program too, but Sunday night services and Sunday school both are lagging way behind in attendance. Is this a common trend?

7. Do the "mega churches" have the traditional SS ministry?

8. I have noticed some of our mission churches do not have Sunday school. Have you noticed that too? If so why do you think that is?

9. Are the Southern Baptist still in the driver's seat when it comes to a growing Sunday school ministry?

10. There are so many things changing in church today as we know it. I fear that Sunday school will soon be a back burner program with Master's Men and CTS. Do fear this is happening too?

11. What basic steps do you think we could take to help revive Sunday school?

12. Does it matter if it is called Sunday school or Small Group Bible Study?

13. How loyal should our churches be to our own publication house?

14. What do you think about D6?

15. Do many or any of our churches (FWB) have part time or full time Christian Ed Directors?

An Oklahoma Teacher stated:

I am happy you addressing the topic of Sunday school and I will take a few minutes to address your questions. I wanted to "vent" a little about Sunday school in that I think it misses a large population that still need Sunday school lessons but perhaps tweaked a little to meet their needs. I feel that believers who are older than 55 are displaced or considered not relevant because of their age. Perhaps they had vigorously served in ministry all of their Christian life but it seems that when we reach a certain age, our experience is dismissed and our ability is overlooked. It is like the young leadership wants to reinvent the wheel in their ministry instead of taking what is known to be tried and true or seek the council of the aged. So much is lost. I know of a great FWB preacher who built great churches and was a tremendous soul winner and is now basically put on the shelf because of age. His wisdom is so valuable to the youth but they don't seem interested in what he knows or has done. To my knowledge, no FWB churches even asks him to speak at special events or to their churches. So much will be lost when these old saints leave this world.

I would like to see literature address this topic: "Just because we get old, we aren't worthless" and keep this in mind when developing literature on how we can still serve even if we are senior citizens. Perhaps there are many old people who would like to serve in some capacity but don't know where or how and are uncertain if it's needed. Perhaps this is why so many old folks don't do anything but attend church. Don't get me wrong. I know aged people are often ill and have health issues that prevents them from serving but perhaps this isn't always the case. Then I would like to see young leadership embrace this fact we still have value not only to God but to the church. It might involve a culture change of the church but personally, it needs to happen.

I put myself and husband in this category I am speaking of. We spent 25 years in contact evangelism and we have a warehouse of experience in dealing with diverse cultures, leading people to the Lord, the discipling of the new believers and become shepherds of the people. If we toss in the other things of an administrative nature including teaching new believers, running organizations, organizing multiple events of religious nature-- well, I believe we could offer some friendly advice to the young leadership. Don't get me wrong. We are in a church where we serve. I write historical Christian plays and my husband and I teach senior citizens on Wed. night but there seem to be no integration of the old people with the youth to where perhaps, the youth could benefit from us and all could work together to build the church. The leadership encourages people to get involved and have their own ministries but I wonder if we old folks would be thought of if a few of us didn't take the time to teach on Wednesday night or Sunday school. I wonder how many SS superintendents are really concerned about what is thought in senior SS classes. I sometimes feel it is burdensome to keep the old people encouraged and involved.

Other topic to consider in teaching senior citizens would be how to deal with illness and loss of a loved one; talk about heaven; grief; and how to continue to serve (I just spoke of that also involves the Pastor's and leaders involvement) to name a few. Encouragement is a great topic too and overcoming disappointments in life perhaps over a loved one or even disappointment with God. There are so many things to consider important for seniors because we are looking at life as well spent. Every day is important on what we do; what we think; and respond.

I hope this doesn't sound like just a venting session but I do believe seniors are displaced somewhat is today's modern churches. Church seems to focus on getting and developing the young couples and families while tossing aside the elderly. We have to change to the changes of the modern church and I think that sometimes it overlooks the needs of the elderly and I have found this to be in more than one church where I have visited or attended.

I am now writing my own curriculum for teaching Wed. nights addressing our founding and using Scriptures and then making a comparison to what is going on in our lives and country today. It is or could be a little controversial but the feedback has been positive and they want me to continue the topic so I guess I will.

A Publisher from Illinois shared:

I am always amazed that minority churches are doing a better job than white churches. Many black churches I work with are still committed to teachers being well prepared before they enter a classroom. Spanish speaking churches are struggling to find male leadership who value SS at all, but in churches who do they thrive best with Spanish materials for their mixed congregations. Asian churches thrive best by infusing their own cultural applications because there is no one "Asian" perspective in translations.

I would try to recapture the evangelistic emphasis and do more to reinforce in attendees that the Bible is the main text book, rather than what is on the best seller list at the bookstore.

A Georgia Minister:

I am glad to see you are still in the fray doing what you can for the success in Sunday schools. I have been here at my church for 15 years now and have had promoted SS and have had campaigns with little success. Would you be willing to talk to me by phone about this? I just preached about the need of Sunday school this past Sunday. If it is like past years there will be very little change in our Sunday school as a result of this message.

A Missouri Teacher:

In our church my role is superficial. I am not allowed to make any decisions except what to order for teachers, nor am I allowed to have any input into what is being planned for SS. I do what I am told and nothing more. (I did have lots of ideas but was told I could not do them in words and in actions.)

A Missouri Teacher:

They are divided in several age groups but you can attend any class you chose. Our Sunday school teacher is a retired English teacher and professor. Most of the teachers do not have that amount of education. Our church refers to Sunday school as Bible Study.

Our Sunday school attendance is about the same number as our regular worship attendance, Early Praise service is half as much. Faith Weaver Friends on Wednesday night has a better attendance than any other service.

I have learned more about the Bible in Sunday school than the regular worship service. My husband has made the same comment.

Through the years I have had the privilege of teaching children in Sunday school and Faith Weaver Friends. I'm always amazed at what the children learn and can remember even though you think sometimes they are not listening.

An Ohio Church officer:

Our SS had good growth <u>when we used to have a structured teacher training and aggressive evangelism outreach ministries.</u>

An Educator in Alabama:

I cannot provide you with some help in the area you are working on, but I am no longer pastoring. When I was, I found that the Sunday school using Denominational literature did not train the students in what was needed to prepare them for service. They used the grasshopper method jumping from one subject to another. I don't suppose I am a good one to inquire of.

A Georgia Pastor:

I have not been able to convince our people on is Sunday school. I have had several campaigns that have only fizzled and embarrassed me. I think our problem boils down to apathy if not outright indifference by 30-40% of our church. I preach a Biblical Christianity based upon regeneration. But, most of the people who have stopped in here for a period of time seems to be satisfied with cheap easy believeism, nominal Christianity, or superficial religiosity, whatever you want to call it. I said in my message this last Lord's Day that people need Sunday school to help disciple them to be an imitator of the Lord Jesus, and to help assimilate them into the family of God.

I have worked with others who are skilled in SS but they have not helped very much. I want our church to be built through the Sunday school, but I am not finding a way to get that done. I am discouraged about our Sunday school and would love to find someone or even a resource that can help us get on the right track.

An Ohio attender:

Growing up a preacher's kid and having been in church and Sunday school since I was knee-high to a grasshopper. I am confident that I have seen about every kind of program and gimmick pastors and promoters could envision. I have been a faithful attendee of Sunday school during much of that time; a teacher for a few years; and presently what I would consider an unfaithful attendee. With that long-time diverse history I believe I have earned the right to critique Sunday school and offer observations as to how impactful it has been in my life and where I see it headed.

From what I understand and have seen personally Sunday school has been on a steady decline for a number of years in all denominations where it still exists. The reasons for the decline are many – some of which can be overcome and some that probably cannot be overcome. The problems with dying Sunday schools echo the problems of dying churches. Painting with a broad brush, one could sum it up by saying that God's plan for the local church has become so far removed by leaders seeking better ways that it no longer accomplishes to any great degree the purpose for which God ordained it – a place to find truth, foster a deeper relationship between oneself and God, and grow together in community.

Church and Sunday school attendance requires an investment of time and energy on the part of the student, teacher and leadership. When a return on investment doesn't yield a sufficient net gain in a reasonable amount of time wise people move in another direction. In a nutshell, that's what happened to Sunday school and church in general from my vantage point. The good teachers stopped putting a lot of time into their lessons relying more on video and book reviews on trendy subjects to fill the SS hour, leadership didn't develop a sufficient replacements and good teachers burned themselves out, and students opted to sleep in and/or get their lesson from other sources. The same sad changes came into pulpits as well.

It doesn't help any either that the world and technology are moving at warp speed offering options for Bible learning and cultivating relationships that never existed before. To complicate matters further the attention span of people is shorter than ever and many simply won't tolerate a mediocre class when they could be spending their time in a place or activity where they perceive a better ROI, even if it is coming from a televangelist in a media-church. Technology and the short attention span it has caused in people is the animal that local churches must learn to deal with because it is here to stay.

Looking back over my 54 years I figure I have invested about 3,000 hours of time in Sunday school. I'd love to have it back because most of it, especially the teen years and up, was usually a waste of time. I was most dissatisfied because it seem I couldn't learn anything new. Often teachers come to class unprepared and lacking Biblical insight. They meant well when accepting a position to teach, but find there is little time left for study with the requirements of work and raising a family.

Nowadays, the problem isn't just in the adult classes. Even kids classes are a joke. We take our 4 year old grandson to church at every opportunity. Sadly, his SS class at our last church needed nothing more than a babysitter. The times I looked in on that class, a Christian cartoon was silently streaming on a monitor as kids played with toys and each other in the floor. I remember as a 4 year old learning Bible verses, hearing Bible stories and flannel-graph lessons. Perhaps it was because my mom was my teacher and I know the work she put into it each week.

As I look back about 30 years, my involvement has been in churches where SS attendance was smaller than attendance for worship and preaching. Prior to that I remember it being vice-versa. That says volumes. People are hungry to know truth and they appear less satisfied when classes are rich in life application lessons and short on deep Bible.

I just left a church where a pastoral change moved a young asst. pastor who wasn't ready to be senior pastor into that position. Because he is young, with a family, active in sports, and busy in the community as a volunteer fire fighter and in local school issues, he's too busy to study a message at any depth. To his credit he is good at attracting new families into the church from his daily activities. No problem there except that their level of Bible knowledge is very shallow. Because he golf's, hunts, camps, and attends sporting events and has no time to study he picks something easy and justifies it by saying he preaches on that level so as not to be over the heads of those who have recently begun attending. An example of a recent sermon was one on the topic of developing friendships. We never opened the Bible in the 30 minutes it took him to preach. To his credit he gave mention to one short Bible verse in passing. My wife and I commented to one another on the way home that we learned a lot about Facebook in that sermon, but we learned nothing about our Lord. A year later, most of those who had scholarly knowledge in that church are gone. Sadly for the new families, there is no other teaching in that church any deeper.

Christians who are studied in the Word no longer have to put up with local pastors of this caliber. One can get simple topical messages or deep expository message from many sources now including the internet and television, not to mention the countless books and learning series available in most Christian bookstores. Because a television show's format demands that they not waste time and get right to the point, I've found there is more solid content in a half hour of good programming than one can get sitting in both SS and a morning sermon.

It's been my experience that preachers and teachers think that people today want topical lessons with three simple points that's easy to recite because they all start with the same letter of the alphabet. I have no idea where that line of thinking came from. They seem to think that expository preaching will kill the crowd, and since it is easier to prepare a topical sermon or lesson than an expository one, it becomes a no-brainer.

I've found the opposite is true, and I personally prefer the content deep so that I will be challenged. As proof of the benefit of deep lessons, Joseph Prince who has the fastest growing church in Singapore with 20,000+ in attendance digs into the Hebrew and Greek in almost every sermon. He demystifies the symbolism in OT offerings and feasts and shows the benefits of the new covenant as opposed to the old. Deep stuff that really makes one appreciate what Jesus did for him/her!

I also get stuff from Robert Morgan, *Christianity Today,* and many others. Getting lessons from the "best of the best" preachers and teachers, and having the option to pick the subject I want to dig into from the convenience of my living room or office is the new form of learning and it makes local sermons and classes seem boring.

An Oklahoma widow:

I'm not attempting to respond to the questions, as our SS is not very praiseworthy at the present. I attend but have no position. One man is supt., adult teacher, etc. and it is down to about 5 people in his adult class. The pastor nor his wife take any part, nor promote it at all. So, my assessment would be pretty pessimistic. But, I know there are many who are doing well.

From a Virginia Pastor:

I find that when I think I am asking God to forgive me I am often in reality...asking Him not to forgive me but to excuse me. But there is all the difference in the world between forgiving and excusing. Forgiveness says 'Yes, you have done this thing, but I accept your apology...' But excusing says 'I see that you couldn't help it or didn't mean it; you weren't really to blame.' ...And if we forget this, we shall go away imagining that we have repented and been forgiven when all that has really happened is that we have satisfied ourselves with our own excuses. They may be very bad excuses; we are all too easily satisfied about ourselves." — C.S. Lewis

Sunday, we will begin working through a new sermon series that will challenge the way you think about the church. No, we won't be trying to re-invent what God already designed perfectly. We will be rethinking through some of our wrong-headed ideas that cause us to short-circuit God's perfect design for the church. So, in this series we will be rethinking the church as:

1. People not a Place
2. Kingdom not Christendom
3. Attractional People, not Attractional Services
4. Disciples not Consumers
5. Pastors not Professionals
6. Multicultural not Mono-cultural
7. Mission not Missions

Why We Axed Sunday school

First of all, let me make it clear that I don't have anything against Sunday school. I grew up on it and I am happy for all the churches that still use it. So, this isn't an axe to grind. This week will be our first Sunday without Sunday school. This is probably the first time in 50+ years that our church will not have the traditional 10:00am Sunday school hour. There are several reasons to discontinue this well-used and well-loved, antiquated relic of the past.

1. it's not in the Bible - I know this may come as a shock to some, but Jesus didn't create Sunday school. Sunday schools were first set up in the 1780s to provide education to working children on their one day off from the factory. It was proposed by Robert Raikes, editor of the Gloucester Journal in an article in his Journal and supported by many clergymen. It aimed to teach the youngsters reading, writing and the knowledge of the Bible. It was a full 90 years in 1870 before children could attend schools during the week. Eventually, D.L. Moody caught on to the concept of Sunday school in the mid-1800 and used it for the same purpose for orphans and homeless children. The church became a place of education for poor kids. Moody's Sunday school became a powerhouse for producing preachers and evangelists! Eventually, the use and function of the Sunday school moved away from an alternate source of education and became simply a designated time of Bible instruction for church goers. In the last 50 years or so, Sunday school became a tool for church growth by dividing people in the church by age groups or affinity groups to attract others of the same demographic. These groups were used to create fellowship among kids, teens, singles, young couples, middle aged couples, and elderly people. In the kind of church I grew up in, the various classes would have contests between each other over who could bring the most visitors. Our church has decided not to use such pragmatic approaches to church growth. I wonder how many people arrived to a Sunday school class just to find out that they were leverage for their friend to win something for having brought them.

What does the Bible say about Sunday school?

The Bible does not mention the Sunday school. The idea of teaching, however, is present in the New Testament Greek word *paideia* and is translated "nurture" in Ephesians 6:4. This word is also translated "instruct" and "chastise" and has the idea of correction and instruction. This is also the purpose of the Word of God. We read in 2 Timothy 3:16-17 that the word of God is profitable for teaching (which is the meaning of the word doctrine), for reproof, for correction and instruction so that the believer is equipped to obey God.

Israel was instructed to teach their children the statutes of the

Lord, and the essence of that teaching is found in Deuteronomy 6:4-7: "Hear O Israel: The LORD our God is One LORD." This is known as the Shema, which is the first word of verse four. Instructions to teach children are also found in Deuteronomy 4:10 and Deuteronomy 11:19. Throughout their history the Jews have conducted, and still conduct, the Yeshiva which is a school for teaching the Torah, the first five books of the Old Testament. It usually began when the child was three to five years old and it was taught only to the boys. That is no longer true. It could be that the Sunday school, which evolved in the evangelical movement, is based upon the premise of the Yeshiva.

We need to remember that in the early years of the church, believers met in homes or caves or areas where they would not be discovered due to persecution. The teaching of God's truth to children was the job of the parents and was done in the home. Sadly, this practice is no longer a priority in the homes of many believers, and many leave the instruction in God's Word to the church and what we now call the Sunday school. But what is taught in Sunday school should only be a supplement to what is taught at home. The ideal situation is when the church and family work together to educate children in the faith.

The Sunday school movement began in Britain in the 1780s and spread to America in the 19th century. But the Sunday schools of that day were nothing like we have today; they were schools very much like our public schools today, only with the Bible as a core component. They were established to provide an elementary education on Sunday for children who were employed in factories, stores, and farms the rest of the week. Eventually, child labor laws were instituted and the institution of the public school was created, relegating religious instruction to the churches. The American Sunday school Union, a cross-denominational national organization founded in Philadelphia in 1824, published curricular materials and children's books that were used in many Sunday schools in that day.

2. Its Institutionalized - Sunday school fit very well into the attractional model of church. The idea of creating a sense of belonging and community through smaller class settings is a great idea that I think is necessary in the church. However, the institutionalized Sunday school re-enforces the message that people can only have fellowship and community at the church building on Sundays. One of the valid complaints raised by the Family Integrated Churches is that Sunday schools have unnecessarily divided the people up into affinity groups that encourage people to only hang out with people of their age group or marital status. When my wife and I were courting, I remember how we used to go out for coffee after the evening services with the elderly people because they were better fellowship than our singles group!

So, in a day and age when the institutionalized church is being more and more distrusted and marginalized, it's probably a good idea to ditch institutions that were not created by God or commanded in the Bible, especially if they become idolized.

3. It Doesn't Work Anymore
The Sunday school stopped functioning as a school a long time ago. Since we have such a mobile culture, we found it was better to have small groups of 8-10 people meeting in each other's homes on different days of the week to study the Bible and fill the need for more fellowship. So, our Sunday school just didn't meet that need anymore. It became just a relic on the church calendar that only those who had been immersed in church-culture were still attending out of habit. Maybe it's my lack of motivational skills, but we couldn't get newer people to attend something that they have to wake up an hour earlier for. The need for teaching is being met on several different opportunities on Sunday and during the week. So we don't need it for that.

Community groups are meeting and having fellowship in people's living rooms rather than in a class room, so we don't need it for that. Sunday school just became obsolete and served no purpose for our church, so we axed it.

If Sunday school still works great for your church...great. Keep it, modify it, and work it! I'm happy for you. But when it becomes nothing more than an extra plate to keep spinning for no reason, pull the plug. It was a method that worked for a while and still works for some, but there's nothing especially holy or faithful by holding on to a tradition that doesn't serve its intended purpose anymore.

Less we forget. Note what a recent national poll revealed:

Two-thirds of the churches identified Sunday school as a contributing or main factor to the churches' evangelistic effectiveness

1

Where Is Your Church's Greatest Health?

Ministry Growth by...
Rethinking the Tradition of Sunday school

The term Sunday school conjures up images of Bible-toting, well-dressed children trooping into classes. It brings back visions of a flannel-graph Apostle Paul (who, interestingly enough, looked exactly like Jonah, Peter, and Saul). It brings back memories of patient and loving teachers, as well as some very fidgety lessons. I look back on Sunday school as a formative factor in my spiritual growth. However, some churches today are dispensing with Sunday school. Is Sunday school an institution we must defend? Or is it something that needs to die?

In order to answer that question, we must think–Scripturally, carefully, prayerfully, and strategically. We need to rethink the cherished tradition of Sunday school.

A. Sunday school – An Evangelistic Success   Way back when Sunday school got started, it was literally just that – an actual school that took place on Sunday. Robert Raikes, a philanthropic and evangelistic newspaper editor started the first Sunday school in 1780. The purpose of his Sunday school was to round up vagabond kids and shuttle them off to a place where they could learn how to read. Most of these children were orphans or street kids, and the other six days of the week they were shut up in the factories of Industrial-Era England. Raikes hoped that Sunday school would help spare them from a future life of crime and indolence. So, he rented some rooms, hired some teachers, and Sunday school was born. The first Sunday schools were not received very well. Since many of them were forced to go, the Street-urchin kids hated having school on their only day off of work. Wild street games were much preferred to stuffy teachers and indecipherable Bibles. The dignified parishioners shared the children's contempt of Sunday school. But their dislike was different; they detested the thought of grimy, sooty, rascals flooding their churches and denigrating the sacred sanctuary. The weary givers who funded the schools feared that their contributions were descending into an ineffective cause. But all that changed. In just a decade from its birth, Sunday school exploded into a phenomenon of evangelistic fervor, reaching millions with the gospel. The Sunday school concept spread from the British Isles to the continent of Europe, infecting Christians with a passion, and affecting the unreached with the gospel. Some church historians look back on the Sunday school movement, and claim that "the starting of Sunday schools saved the church from extinction." To say that Sunday school was "successful" is to understate its impact.

Sunday school

– An Evangelistic Success

Sunday school today

Sunday school today is vastly different from Sunday school in 1780. Everything about it has changed–except for the fact that it takes place on Sunday. The motive has changed. The financial support has changed. The administration has changed. The structure has changed. The style has changed. The goal has changed. The attendance has changed. The audience has changed. Over the course of 245 years, Sunday school has morphed into an altogether different event. 245 years will change things.

Change is not evil. But when change happens—intentionally or unintentionally—one must determine whether that change is positive or negative. One should not necessarily gaze backwards to try to restore something to its original form. Over the shoulder wistfulness degenerates into anachronistic ineffectiveness. Instead, one must look at an issue from three perspectives.

> Past:
> Understand the history.
> Present:
> Understand the present form.
> Future:
> Envision the long-term goal.

1).Past: Understand the history.
2).Present: Understand the present form.
3).Future: Envision the long-term goal.

This kind of strategic thinking needs to be rooted in a solid mission and vision. A church without a mission is like an oar with holes. You will row forever, but never get anywhere. A biblically-derived mission and vision is the crucial starting point for ministry strategizing.

B. The Challenges of Sunday school
So, what is Sunday school today?

Sunday school lacks a great commission focus. Rather than

functioning with the goal of making disciples, Sunday school is often in a maintenance mode.

- Sunday school depends on published curriculum from the 'experts.' Sunday school curriculum is the bread-and-butter of some major publishing houses. Rather than understanding and adapting to the unique needs of their congregation, Sunday school depends on printed material or booklets from outside sources.

- Sunday school separates the family by age-indexing. Is the age-indexing of the church healthy? It almost goes without questioning today that a church needs to have a separate room, class, teacher, and curriculum for every age category. However, at closer inspection, the effect that age-indexing has on the family does not seem right. Is this really necessary, beneficial, and in keeping with the biblical paradigm for the family? Must we separate the Christian family every Sunday—at a time where they should be worshiping together?

- Sunday school curriculum often prescribes moralism, to the neglect of strategic evangelism. Usually, this happens in children's classes, where teaching major biblical concepts and spirituality is challenging. However, it can happen for all age categories. Patrick, in his book *The Church Planter*, said it best: "For many American churches the focus has been almost exclusively on converting people to a code of Christian conduct with the hope that they will 'behave' their way to salvation. This couldn't be further from the intent of the gospel of grace."

- Sunday school programs often lack a long-term plan. Many Sunday schools go into 'existence mode,' maintaining a tradition without posturing for productivity. The result is a semester-by-semester approach or a topic-by-topic approach to Sunday school planning, rather than a big-picture vision for discipleship.

There are more than just this list of woes of Sunday school. The point of this chapter is not to bash Sunday school. The point is to *think* about Sunday school. The point is to help you determine whether your efforts toward Sunday school are more like feeding a stray pet or healthy work horse.

C. A Barrage of Considerations

So, here comes the artillery–a barrage of questions, statements, and aphorisms to help you think about Sunday school.

a. Just because Sunday school has been successful in the past, doesn't mean it's going to be successful in the future. Keep the three-perspective principal when rethinking Sunday school (not the backwards-only look). If something *has been* successful, it is necessary for that thing to continually modify, adapt, and regroup to maintain its impact. This takes strategic thinking, prayerful consideration, and bold moves.

b. Don't dispense with something simply for the sake of being cool or contemporary. Only dispense with something if it is truly a distraction or violation to the purposes of God and the goal of the church. If Sunday school needs to bite the dust, then kill it. If Sunday school is effectively ministering to the needs of the people, and fulfilling a Great Commission role (both evangelism *and* discipleship) then keep it.

c. Don't idolize traditions. Tradition can turn into idolatry. It may happen that someone in the church—be it a pastor, deacon, or member—breathes the slightest hint of change: "Should we keep the Sunday school program?" There are those in the church who may view such a question as an outright attack on the faith! Doing away with Sunday school is nearly tantamount to eradicating the church or denying the existence of God. The illustration is intentionally overstated, but do you see the point? If Sunday school is so near and dear to the faith, then why don't we see it clearly in the Bible? When we begin cherishing traditions above the inspired Word of God, we make a tragic mistake. When we think that our man-made institutions are more important than strategic adaption and biblical innovation, we are treading into dangerous territory.

d. Rethink your non-negotiable. Every ministry has them, whether they are written down or not. They're called non-negotiables. What are the most important features of your ministry—features that you will not compromise? To derive such non-negotiables, go to the Scripture. Then write them down. Ministries without "non-negotiables," "distinctives," "essentials," or whatever they're called, are likely to idolize tradition and cling to the past. They make tradition their non-negotiable.

e. Form a mission and vision statement. In a future post, we will discuss the why and how of a mission and vision statement. For now, simply understand that a mission and vision statement are both the compass and the engine for your ministry. In order to know where you're going, you must have a vision (compass). In order to mobilize and motivate for action, you must have a mission (engine).

f.   There is such a thing as positive change. As we discussed above, not all change is evil. Change—even painful, difficult, and opposition-motivating change—can be a good thing. Sometimes, things just need to die. And it may be a good thing. If you face opposition to a decision to change, it doesn't mean that the decision is wrong. In fact, it may just mean the opposite. A. W. Tozer said, "To be right with God has often meant to be in trouble with men." Eliminating Sunday school will not create a ministry vacuum. Instead, it may free the church to do more...to do better.

g.   Practice asking *why*. "Why?" is a powerful question. It is a life-changing question. Asking "why" can change the course of a ministry, a life, or a nation. When you turn the floodlight of this question onto Sunday school, it may be very revealing. Mustering up answers to the "why" question isn't done by merely brainstorming. It's done by going to the Scripture. If you can derive Scriptural motivations for the existence of Sunday school, great. If not, keep asking why. Then change. Ask why again. Change some more. Keep asking why. Keep changing. But keep Scripture at the center of your questioning *and* your changing.

It's time to put our minds to better use. As leaders, pastors, volunteers, or church members, we know too well the daily grind. Our gaze is always on the here-and-now. Our energies are being expended to try to put one foot in front of the other. Can we take some of that energy to look up, to look ahead? When our thinking is entrenched in the day-to-day maintenance of ministry, we rarely take the time to forge ahead and evaluate our present ministry. And what's happening? We're compromising maximum effectiveness. "Rethinking" is hard work. But the really hard work comes not in the rethinking, but in the retooling,–in taking those thoughts and strategies and implementing them for God's glory

I believe wholeheartedly there are non-Scriptural traditions (traditions that are not directly ordered in the Scriptures) should always be under scrutiny; and also that just because something served some function in the past that it is not wrong for it to serve another function now, necessarily.

I believe wholeheartedly there are non-Scriptural traditions (traditions that are not directly ordered in the Scriptures) should always be under scrutiny; and also that just because something served some function in the past that it is not wrong for it to serve another function now, necessarily. I think the two functions that Sunday school have served (excluding the very first reason), that of evangelism and education have to be realized in your church in some way or the other, by New Testament Scriptural demand/command. If you want to abandon Sunday school that serves one of the purposes for a stronger conveyance of serving the evangelism and/or education purposes, then have something in place more viable, more likely to be supported by your church and your community. It could be small groups in homes, bible courses in your church, evangelism rallies, or whatever.

II.   Another Look At Sunday school

A few years back I heard Rev. B. L. Efird, an associate of an active Church, with an outstanding Sunday school in Inman, South Carolina, present the following seminar.

While many churches are considering Sunday schools a tool of the past. A church in Inman, SC is using the power of the Sunday school to build a strong and vibrant church. There is much to learn about the effective use of the Sunday school.

Have you ever really thought about what Sunday school should be like? If you could design your own Sunday school class, how would it be? Would it be a Sunday school where people look forward to attending because they will get help in their Christian life? Will they meet and talk with friends? Will they have fun times with friends?

Would it be a Sunday school that people actually try to get their unchurched friends to attend with them? Would it be Sunday school that causes people to get up on Sunday morning, excited about participating in Bible study? Would it be a Sunday school where group members care about and feel responsible for their fellow group members who are hurting or absent?

Perhaps you have not known of such a Sunday school. In light of reality, such an existence would seem a dream world. Yet, there is no reason why such a Sunday school could not exist. In fact, with God's approval and guidance, there is no reason why every Sunday school could not be like this one!

Consequently, because of the death of so many Sunday schools over recent decades, many are prone to consider the Sunday school to be dead if not a necessary evil. Ralph L. McIntyre writes, "The only people who think that Sunday school is dead or dying are those who are dead or dying, spiritually."

The Biblical basis for Sunday school still exists and can be found as early as Deuteronomy 31:12, 13. *Gather the people together, men, and women, and children, and thy stranger that is within thy gates, that they may hear, and that they may learn, and fear the LORD your God, and observe to do all the words of this law: And that their children, which have not known anything, may hear, and learn to fear the LORD your God, as long as ye live in the land whither ye go over Jordan to possess it.* One obvious reason for Sunday school is that it can be a vehicle for teaching the fear of God to every age. The neglect of this mandate has, for the most part, been the contributing factor that has led much to the moral decline of America. To turn it around would involve the efforts of every fundamental, Bible-believing, preaching, soul-winning church in America!

In this brief article I would like to share two principles that can help us develop a mind set for a growing Sunday school.

A. Grab the Vision

We must first of all believe that it is God's will for the church (your church) to grow! I am convinced that the vehicle God is using to build our church and many others is that of the Sunday school. Dr. Elmer Towns, a leading authority in church growth, has said, "I believe God will continue to use the Sunday school as the evangelistic and educational arm of the church."

The reasons for a growing Sunday school are numerous. *"Until we all know and practice everything that there is to learn from the Bible, we will need Sunday schools"* (Ralph L. McIntyre).

Churches are built on relationships of people, and the Sunday school provides the greatest basis for developing and building close-knit relationships. A recent poll concerning what

ഇഇ

Gather the people together, men, and women, and children, and thy stranger that is within thy gates, that they may hear, and that they may learn, and fear the LORD your God, and observe to do all the words of this law: And that their children, which have not known anything, may hear, and learn to fear the LORD your God, as long as ye live in the land whither ye go over Jordan to possess it.

Deuteronomy 31:12, 13.

ഇഇ

influences people to go to church reveals the following:

Advertisements...2%
Organized Visitation...6%
Pastoral Contact...6%
Invitation from a Friend...86%

Dr. Elmer Towns concludes that for every member of the Sunday school or church, there are at least ten prospective members within that one person's web of relationships.

It is plain to see that the Sunday school is not only the great social arm of the church, but that it can also be the church's greatest arm of outreach. The greatest influence is often among the laity who are scattered abroad in the various work forces, schools, clubs, and many other social organizations. When activated through an effective Sunday school outreach procedure, the Sunday school can become the greatest tool of evangelism in the church! With outreach now organized and implemented, the Sunday school can continue in becoming the most effective base for discipleship. It can provide the best means of teaching, equipping, and assimilating converts into local church ministries.

Dr. Elmer Towns concludes that for every member of the Sunday school or church, there are at least ten prospective members within that one person's web of relationships.

In short, the Sunday school becomes the church organized. Organization, in the truest sense, is nothing more than being in the best possible position to be used by the Holy Spirit. When organized properly, the Sunday school provides the organizational structure for the development and maintenance of any and all church ministries. In effect, every basic need of the church can be met through a properly organized Sunday school.

Reason Why Your Sunday school Can and Will Grow

God wants your Sunday school to grow (Deuteronomy 31:12, 13). God wants us to share Him with others, and what better way to teach people about Him than through the Sunday school? God in His Word declares that He will grant our hearts' desire in accordance to His will. And if we desire for the Sunday school to grow numerically and spiritually, it will by God's help if we let Him. First John 3:22 declares, "And whatsoever we ask, we receive of Him, because we keep His commandments, and do those things that are pleasing in His sight."

Reason Why Your Sunday School Cannot And Will Not Grow

Your Sunday school cannot and will not grow so long as you listen to the devil's lie that somehow spirituality goes hand-in-hand with smallness. There is no spiritual blessing in remaining small! God wants us to prosper in His work. Psalm 1:3 declares that whatever the godly man does will prosper. We are advised in 3 John: 2 that above all things it is hoped that we will prosper. Mark 11:24 states that whatever we desire when we pray, if we believe, we shall have our desire!

Change IS NOT superficial, temporary behavior modification
Change IS the Holy Spirit's alteration of one's heart.

Your Sunday school cannot and will not grow unless you have a desire to grow. Psalm 37:3-5 admonishes us to "Trust in the Lord, and do good; so shalt thou dwell in the land, and verily thou shalt be fed. Delight thyself also in the Lord; and he shall give thee the desires of thine heart. Commit thy way unto the Lord; trust also in him; and he shall bring it to pass." To desire growth in the Sunday school means to pray for growth. It means to believe in growth. It means to work for growth. Desire means to concentrate on success and refuse to accept mediocrity and failure. The reason a lot of folks are failing, especially when it comes to Sunday school, is because they are working at it. One of the foremost problems that a person must face in a small or dying Sunday school is a lack of interest. When something is dead or lacks interest or fails to meet the needs of people, it becomes boring. When a lack of interest infects the laity, it is serious; when it occurs in the ministry of the church, it is disastrous. It is imperative that the pastor, staff, and laity all be enthused about the project growth and its expected results.

B. Structure Your Sunday school for Growth

A healthy structure for any Sunday school begins with a Mission or Purpose Statement. Such a statement should be based on both the Great Commission (Matthew 28:18-20) as well as the Great Commandment (Matthew 22:37-39).

The development of a Vision Statement will allow the participant to form a clear picture and an accurate understanding of God, himself, and his circumstances.

A healthy structure for any Sunday school begins with a Mission or Purpose Statement. Such a statement should be based on both the Great Commission (Matthew 28:18-20) as well as the Great Commandment
(Matthew 22:37-39)

Once vision is established, Realistic Goals must be set. Goals are detailed targets that will accomplish both vision and purpose. Goals must be SMART: Specific, Measurable, Attainable, Realistic, and Time-bound.   With goals set you are now ready to plan your Strategy. This is a detailed course or action that moves the Sunday school to achieve goals.

Developing a set of Core Values is next on the growth agenda. Core Values reflect what a congregation believes. A lack of core values creates undue stress and leads the way for failure to develop one's life on the foundation of Biblical principles. Over 60 percent of Evangelicals polled said they did not believe in absolute truth!

The development of Lay Leadership and Lay Ministry is essential for a Great Commission Sunday school. The 20-80 Principle of Church Growth suggests that in order to grow, the pastor must invest 80 percent of his time developing leadership skills within the 20 percent who produce 80 percent of the results. Once the 20 percent develops leadership within themselves they can begin to influence the 80 percent who will then become participants rather than spectators. Thus new workers are enlisted who enhance the overall growth of the Sunday school through the creation of new units and ministries along with new personnel and leadership.

C. The Need and Process of Genuine Change

From time to time we are approached by folks who are looking for real solutions to their problems. Whether they come purposefully or only in general conversation, the fact is, they are looking to us because we are **believers**. Sadly, many times we do not take advantage of these opportunities to minister. We are all too often ill-prepared to really offer meaningful help.

1. We Have a Biblical Mandate

Part of the Great Commission is teaching others *to observe all things* that the Lord has commanded (Mt. 28:20). In other words, it is our obligation as mature believers to disciple those around us. Paul commanded, *Let the word of Christ dwell in you richly in all wisdom; teaching and admonishing one another...* (Col. 3:16). The idea here is to lovingly confront one another with the truth.

Believers should influence others in two basic ways:

Evangelism (Mt. 28:19-20).   GOAL = Salvation
Edification (1 Th. 5:11ff).   GOAL = Sanctification

2. We Have a Biblical Method

Many people will say that they want to change, but what do they mean? Just as the word "food" could mean anything from a Pop-Tart to Prime Rib, so we may have varying ideas about change.

When we speak of change we are talking about movement either away from God (sin) or movement toward God (sanctification). True change, then, does not come from turning over a new leaf, but from "a systematic series of actions." It is a process of growing towards God. Our method is condensed for us in 2 Timothy 3:14-17:

But continue thou in the things which thou hast learned and hast been assured of, knowing of whom thou hast learned them; And that from a child thou hast known the Holy Scriptures, which are able to make thee wise unto salvation through faith which is in Christ Jesus. All scripture is given by inspiration of God, and is profitable for doctrine, for reproof, for correction, for instruction in righteousness: That the man of God may be perfect, thoroughly furnished unto all good works (2 Tim. 3:15-17)

Holy Spirit changes the human heart through the Word of God. We often affirm our allegiance to the Bible as the inerrant, infallible rule of faith and practice; but if that were true we would readily submit to it whether we liked it or not.

Let's be reminded of some important truths about the Bible:

Holy.
In other words, it is set apart. See 2 Pet. 1:21.
Able.
Literally, it "has the power."   See Rom. 15:4.
Inspired.
Literally, it is "God breathed."
Profitable.
The bible is useful to accomplish something beneficial.
Sufficient.
We need not turn anywhere else. See 2 Pet. 1:3.

3. We have a Biblical Obligation. (Mt. 28:19)

Step #1: Communication

All scripture is given by inspiration of God, and is profitable for doctrine. The word is actually teaching.

Teach others to observe God's Word. Prepare to instruct. We are to be both students of the Word (1 Tim. 4:15ff) and stewards of the Word (2 Tim. 2:15)

The Object of the Teacher

The end of communicating the Word. Times and cultures are different, painting different pictures of what we are to be; but God's Word is immutable, and paints an unchanging portrait of the believer! The Bible must always be held high. It is the standard, and for that we do not have to apologize.

1. Christ-likeness is produced in the life of the believer. By communicating the Word we demonstrate two things: what we need to be and how we must become it.
2. Confidence in the Word of God is evidenced, and not in self or in the helper.

The means of communicating the Word.

1. Communication requires a personal involvement.
2. Communication requires discovering the real problem.
3. Communication requires a clear exposition of a biblical passage addressing the need.

Step #2: Conviction

All scripture is given by inspiration of God, and is profitable for doctrine, for reproof (2 Tim. 3:16). Conviction is an essential step in true, biblical change. It follows logically from realizing what God requires. The order cannot be reversed. For example see Acts 2   Neh. 8.

Three Instruments of Conviction

- The Spirit Convicts (John 16:8)
- The Scripture Convicts (2 Tim. 3:16)
- The Saint Convicts (2 Tim. 4:2)

Putting these three together, we can summarize it this way: The **saint** must communicate the **Scripture** in the power of the **Spirit** with a view to bringing conviction.

The Importance of Conviction

Care for His children (Heb. 12:5-11).

Other Issues in Conviction

o   By definition, **sin is *the transgression of the law*** (1 Jn. 3:4b). There can be great conviction as a result of simply teaching the requirements of God.

- o Always express conclusions in biblical terminology.

- o Calling sin **"sin"** gives hope.

- o Do not **accuse** people of sinning who have not sinned.

- Put responsibility where it belongs. The current trend is to be a victim. But even having suffered at the hand of someone else does not excuse sinful responses (Rom. 12:14-21).

  - o Bring folks to conviction with their **own mouth** (2 Sam. 12).

Step #3: Correction

All scripture is given by inspiration of God, and is profitable for doctrine, for reproof, for correction (2 Tim. 3:16). The Greek word translated "correction" means to stand up straight — especially after a fall. This picture could be seen in the ancient world when a helmsman on a ship would correct his course on the basis of feedback from his other shipmates. So our goal as believers is not only to expose the wrongs, but also to right them.

We can do this by giving a person honest, loving feedback, which most people never receive. Generally, in the name of love, people often give misleading, dishonest assessments of a person's life. This is NOT the loving action of a believer! If you do not provide them with accurate feedback, how will they have the proper information necessary to correct their course? So correction is the pivotal point of change, in which we adjust our way of thinking and living from unbiblical to biblical.

Rethinking Your Course

The key to this discussion is repentance. Not many really understand what biblical repentance is, and even fewer practice it as they navigate through life. The word literally means to rethink. It is the review of one's behavior, attitudes, and beliefs; it is arriving at a new viewpoint, so that a person's lifestyle must change.

Repentance is NOT simply the expression of regret or some emotional remorse, as can be seen in the lives of Judas (Mt. 27:3) and Esau (Heb. 12:17). Broadly speaking, a person regrets being caught. He is sorry because of the consequences of his actions, not because those actions were sins against God. In these cases what is missing is godly sorrow (**See 2 Cor. 7:8-12**).

The evidence of repentance in the Bible is not regret, but fruit. John the Baptist insisted that his hearers *bring forth fruits worthy of* [or meet for] *repentance* (**See Lk. 3:8-14**). John commanded not only that their besetting sin be abandoned, but that they also adopt the corresponding positive fruit of the Spirit.

- Confession of the Sin (Pr. 28:13).
- Forgiveness for the Sin (1 Jn. 1:7, 9).
- Forsaking the Sin (Mt. 5:27-30).
- Amending the Course.

Step #4: Continuation in Righteousness

All scripture is given by inspiration of God, and is profitable for doctrine, for reproof, for correction, for instruction in righteousness: *that the man of God may be perfect, thoroughly furnished unto all good works* (2 Tim. 3:16-17).

The word translated *instruction* is literally disciplined training, much like that of a child. Fathers are taught to raise their children *in the nurture and admonition of the Lord* (Eph. 6:4). The word *nurture* is the same as *instruction*. It is the idea of discipline with teeth. The OT concept is similar. It is "correction which results in education." This type of instruction can be painful, likened to the strenuous exercise of athletes, but it is beneficial to those who endure (see Heb. 12:5-7).

Now that the sin has been corrected, we have to now prepare him for the future. He needs training as to what to expect ahead and how to respond in that situation. If no further instruction is given, if no proper training is provided, he will respond the way he has always responded. He will sin again and get discouraged over his failure.

The Goal of the Instruction

Remember, there is a goal in all of this. We want to guide our brother or sister to become a *perfect* (or complete) person, furnished unto all good works. Paul uses the word righteousness to describe the goal (we have previously called it Christ-likeness). In this case, we are not talking about our position in Christ, but our progression in Christ. That is, we are learning to do the right thing, as we yield our hearts to the Spirit of God.

Getting from Point A to Point B

In Romans 6 we are given some powerful, needful instruction that will help in this area. In this passage we learn several things:

- Believers *should walk in the* newness *of life* (v.4).
- Believers *should not* serve *sin*; they have been *freed from sin* (v.6-7).
- Sin should not *reign in your mortal body that ye should obey it in the lusts thereof.* (v.12).
- Believers should *yield* to God (v.13), become *the servants of righteousness* (v.18).
- Believers then produce fruit *unto holiness* (v.22).

So to bear the fruits of righteousness and to be servants of righteousness, we have to be instructed in righteousness. We have to learn to "put off" the old man and "put on" the new man. We are replacing bad habits with godly ones.

The key is helping a person to learn new habits to take the place of the ones that were corrected. A large part of our lives is done habitually. A habit is a blessing from God that enables us to do things unconsciously, automatically, skillfully, and comfortably. Sadly, however, fallen man has corrupted habits that must be changed. See Eph. 4:22ff.

Often that means running a person through scenarios biblically and thoughtfully. When we do this we are conditioning them to respond in a godly way when they are then placed in that particular situation. For instance, how would you instruct a teenager or young adult who is prone to promiscuity? Use example of Joseph in Potiphar's house

It takes this kind of spiritual "boot camp" to really make a long-lasting change. We must not be content with a single decision, but follow up with regular discipleship that promotes continual righteousness.

Sunday school is so exciting, it offers another opportunity (like bible study) to discuss, read out loud, share opinions and truths, and teach the Word of God at a more one on one level. Our ministry would not get rid of this awesome tool that was given years ago. It is refreshing, we find people who would never say anything or get a chance to express themselves come alive in Sunday school and become wiser, more into the word of God. I think many churches are trying stay so modern for the young folk but we must let the young people adjust to Christianity, change is good, but we can overdo it.

Things in the Church that cannot Change

I can tell you seven things in the church that should not change. In the fast pace of change in local congregations, these seven constants are good reminders of what really matters.

The Bible is still the Word of God. It always has been and always will be. It is sharper than a two-edged sword. It is powerful because it is the Word of God.

The gospel still changes lives. The gospel is the power unto salvation. The gospel transforms lives. The gospel is the same regardless of other changes in our churches.

Small groups are still vital. In the New Testament, groups sometimes met together in homes or other places. Throughout Church history, the role of groups has been vital. It is the place where community is established and where deep truths are taught. It has been called Sunday school, small groups, home groups, and cell groups. But they are all forms of small groups creating community and fellowship and learning.

The mission field still needs workers. That includes the mission fields to the farthest ends of the earth. And it includes the community in our backyard.

Prayer is still powerful. God is still using praying churches. Never, ever take for granted the power of pervasive prayer.

Hurting people still need ministry. Pain and hurt may come in different names over the years, but the needs are still similar. A church that truly cares for people will always have a place in the community. A church that sees people through the eyes of Jesus will always be effective.

God is still in control. Sometimes the pace of change confuses and disorients us. Sometimes the amount of suffering in the world challenges us. Sometimes we feel like there is no hope. Remember, God is still in control. He always has been; He always will be. He is there for you and your church.

2

How Healthy Is Your Churches Biblical Knowledge?

Ministry Growth by Knowledge...
What Growing Churches
Have In Common

It is easy think about the "church of the good old days." Remember Sunday singings? Two week revivals? How quickly we forget shallow spiritual growth, negligent ministry, and personality problems! Quite frankly, the "glory days" of potluck dinners and homemade altars were not as glamorous as some believe. Problems existed in the church then and problems exist in the church now. I'm afraid the church of the future will encounter many of the same problems if we fail to learn from mistakes made in the past! One such mistake we cannot afford to make is the failure to meet the needs of the changing and hurting society around us.

God fully expects the church of Jesus Christ to be a shining light in the midst of a dark and hostile world. In recent years, however, many Christians have dropped the ball. This must stop! It is not only possible but necessary for the church to be in contact with the world without becoming like the world. The church was never intended to be isolated from the culture in which it exists. How can the church today meet the needs of 21st century American culture? We must meet several difficult challenges and overcome them with the strength and wisdom of God. What are these challenges?

- Our aging society
- The difficulty the Church has in reaching and keeping youth
- Ethnicity changes will affect the church
- The moral breakdown of our society
- The disappearance of doctrine

Our Aging Society

The 2010 census found 319 million people in the United States. Two hundred fifty-four million (81%) are adults. The 65+ age group has outnumbered teens since December 1983. The teen population is only 22 million, while those who are 65 and older number 84 million. More than one half of all people who have ever lived beyond 65 live today! The over 65 group is multiplying three times faster than the rest of the population, which makes it the fastest growing age group. By 2010 the number of seniors in the United States had doubled. In that same year, one fourth of all Americans were more than 65 years old. Even more startling, one out of every four senior citizens have children who are over 65.

How can the church minister more effectively to an aging society?

Provide for their spiritual growth! Churches today often emphasize ministry to children and teens while the needs of seniors are overlooked or taken for granted. The truth is, today's churches should have a minimum of three adult Sunday school classes to each teen or children's class simply because the adult population is so large, and it is growing larger all the time.

Give them opportunities for ministry. Life expectancy for men and women today is 78 and 84 . . . and rising quickly. The 2010 census found 68,000 Americans over 100 years old, an increase of more than 38,000 since 1990. These valuable members of the church should not be forgotten! They need and want a place to volunteer their talents. We must tap the potential of those in our aging congregations.

Recognize their financial faithfulness. This "over the hill" group has more advantages than any generation society has ever known. They benefit from Social Security, which began in their lifetime. They grew up during the early mutual fund era, invested in the stock market, and established retirement programs at work. In fact, those between ages 55-65 own 70% of the nation's financial assets. More than 80% travel for leisure and 48% buy luxury cars. It is likely that this age group will live in assisted living centers rather than in the poorer nursing homes of times past. However, this group has proven to be faithful to God with the blessings He has given them.

It is evident that our aging society will become the means of financial support for the church. They have a history of contributing faithfully to the church. Statistics reveal that middle-aged and younger adults make smaller and less frequent contributions. Even those churches that cater to younger members are often supported by their seasoned and mature members.

The Difficulty the Church Has Reaching and Keeping Youth

Today, there are 22 million teens in the U.S. This age group faces many challenges as they seek to deal with the social problems of the last three decades—problems that have culminated in a generation in shambles. Divorce has contributed to the struggles of children and teens. The statistics regarding children of divorced parents are alarming. They are more likely to be divorced, go to jail, not believe in God, work a low paying job, drop out of school, nor own a home.

Of the 22 million teens in our society, 800,000 to one million are currently in jail or in prison.

- These troubled children are the products of a

hurting and sin-damaged society!

- Ten percent of all children and teens under the age of 18 have grown up in a single parent home.
- Parents hand over 20 billion dollars a year to children under the age of 18 with very little supervision or accountability.
- The top problems among teens today are: drug abuse, alcohol abuse, pregnancy, suicide, rape, robbery and assault.
- Disconnected from adults, many teens display a bully mentality and a violent nature. They are influenced more by technology than by their parents, yet the literacy rate among young people is dropping steadily! Teens are spiritual, but it is without limits, and they are likely to believe anything that helps them at the time. Resistant to a world controlled by an aging society, children and teens feel adults are out of touch. They increasingly distrust authority, and often make decisions without any thought for consequences.

Of our present teen community only 20% come from stable homes, while 60% may experience broken homes or are from those with "normal" problems, and the remaining 20% are among those at high risk sociologically. How can the church hope to meet the needs of such a challenging generation?

It will NOT be easy. Churches must bridge the age and cultural gap that exists between generations. Diverse music styles, the inability to read an older English Bible, and a general lack of communication have created a broad chasm between the aging church and today's students with little tolerance from either side. Churches must take the steps needed to communicate to this new breed of American. She must adapt principles of cross-cultural ministry: understanding the culture,

Special

More than 636 languages are spoken in the U.S. 39% do not speak any English

and enduring problems with patience!

However, today's church must not lose hope! One of the new and quickly-growing frontiers for the church is the 20-35 age group, formerly the most unreached group in America. While atheism and secularism are strong in this age group, many are returning to church, looking for the answers that education and wealth did not give them. And they are bringing their children back to church. In the early 1990's an unexpected baby boom gave new life to the aging church. As a result, the primary and junior age groups are growing. They must not be forgotten for they will be the foundation of the church in future generations.

Finally, the church must give today's students opportunities to be involved in the church—from worship and outreach to organization and giving. It is only when today's children and teens feel a part of the church, and see the church as a vital and relevant part of their lives that they will truly give themselves to the ministry of the church.

Ethnicity Changes Will Affect the Church

The last few years have seen great changes take place among the differing minorities of our country. More than 636 languages are spoken in the U.S. In fact, some estimates claim that as much as 39% of the American population does not speak English. To find a school system without multiple languages very rare. These changes are affecting the church. I sat in my seat at church recently and beside me sat four from the Philippines. I looked across the auditorium and noticed Hispanics, Orientals, Native Americans and Anglo-Americans from nearly every country in Europe. Have we forgotten we were once from another land and like them seeking new hope?

During the last century, 83% of those who immigrated to the U.S. came from Europe; today, however, 75% of our immigrants come from the Pacific Rim and Latin America. Our newest citizens come from non-Christian countries—countries with non-biblical, pagan religions. The Asian-American community is growing faster than any other race in American society, and Asian-Americans are better educated than all other segments of our society. When the Asian community becomes the largest minority group, the Anglo-American community will become an official minority. Most social analysts estimate that European-Americans will be a minority by the year 2050. How can the American church, with its large concentration of Anglo-Americans, have a vital outreach to the growing influx of immigrants?

We must overcome our prejudices! Anglo-Americans have not outgrown their prejudices toward other people groups. Many times, people of other races are treated like "second class citizens" by our churches. We must embrace new believers from other cultures as precious members of the body of Christ, forgetting our cultural differences as we worship Christ!

The Disappearance of Doctrine

Forty years ago, 90% of churchgoers were faithful to a specific church or denomination because they believed in the doctrines taught by that church. Today 60% of those visiting a church come with little or no understanding of ANY church doctrine.

This problem is complicated by an American culture that has moved the Christian God out of its consciousness. The media portrays a culture devoid of any meaningful Christian content or practice.

On campuses and in the media, the only absolutes these days is that there are no absolutes. Morality is radically individual, as people decide what is right or wrong with no standard to go by but their own feelings and wishes.

Today's world and our lives are driven by technology. Many live most of their days alone with a machine. Increasingly people prefer to communicate electronically because it is safer and very controlled. As a result, life is impersonal and often empty. We communicate more than ever, yet we have never been more isolated. Individualistic and self-serving modern Americans are cut off from the community and family.

The church faces a drastic change in ministry focus. Many churches are comfortable to worship in the suburbs, among people that look like them, in a worship style that is familiar and traditional. The truth is, as we plan for the future, the church must take cities, styles, and cultures into consideration if we plan to reach these new Americans with the gospel. What a challenge if the church is to survive! Perhaps that is why it is called the GREAT Commission!

The Moral and Social Breakdown of Our Society

In many ways, today's society is crumbling just outside the walls of the church! Did you know that today 50% of Americans are single? This group, those who have never married, widows, widowers, and the divorced presents a daunting challenge to the 21st century church. The number of widows and widowers continues to grow in our society. As mentioned previously, countless numbers of marriages end in divorce, and according to some reports, almost half of all adults under the age of 30 lived with their partner before marriage. Commitment to marriage is at an all-time low. Today those of the 20-40 age group approach marriage believing they will divorce before they say I do—not just once, but three times!

Crime, social unrest and race-related violence is on the rise while integrity falls by the wayside. Politicians caught red-faced in scandals are no longer regarded with disgust but become the source of amused conversation. Jails are full, cults are thriving, and abortion claims the lives of millions of unborn babies every year. It's NOT a pretty picture. Does the church have any hope of making a difference?

No! Not as long as we continue to bury our heads in the sand. No! Not as long as we refuse to get our hands dirty, content to sit in the quiet solitude of our sanctuaries No! Not until we learn to widen our circle of acquaintances to include those who make us uncomfortable. No! Not until we cast off the pride that would keep us from sharing Christ with those we consider "below our social standing."

Learn from the Savior, who never denied or avoided the failures of His culture, but who faced sin head on, face to face . . and changed lives.

Consumerism is the engine that drives our culture. The subtle dangers of materialism/consumerism may be the most deadly enemies of the church, because most of us naively accept their grip on our lives. We live in an adversarial world, and all of us take the conflict home and to church. Racial, ethnic, gender, generational, family, and political battles dot the cultural map of our time.

Downsizing, re-engineering, and an obsolescent workforce are creating insecurity that has many younger Americans thinking they will experience downward mobility. American people are increasingly pessimistic, as American culture virtually disintegrates before their eyes. And in the mist of this broken world, the church has forgotten the biblical doctrine that gives people something to believe in, something to cling to when troubles come their way.

Many of the nearly 420 mega-churches scattered across the United States offer a generalized and loose curriculum. Much of their teaching meets a temporary need with little long time satisfaction. In an effort to please everyone, they fail to satisfy anyone spiritually. Today we are in a new era. Most call it a new mindset—Postmodernism.

In his book *The Death of Truth,* Dennis McCallum explains this new mindset in our time. "Postmodernism isn't a distinct set of doctrines or truth claims. It's a **mood**—a view of the world characterized by a deep distrust of reason, not to mention a disdain for the knowledge Christians believe the Bible provides. It's a **methodology**—a completely new way of analyzing ideas. For all its diverse ideas and advocates, postmodernism is also a **movement**—a fresh onslaught on truth that brings a more or less cohesive approach to literature, history, politics, education, law, sociology, linguistics, and virtually every other discipline, including science. And it is ushering in a cultural **metamorphosis**—transforming every area of everyday life as it spreads through education, movies, television, and other media." I honestly believe that many problems in our present society have come about because the church has ceased to carry out her responsibility to teach the Word of God.

We live in a day when the church most needs to be the church! As Christians, we need to let people know what we believe and do our best to help them deal with life's problems based on the framework of the Word of God. Saint Boniface (A.D. 680-754) once said, "The church is like a great ship being pounded by the waves of life's different stresses. Our duty is not to abandon ship, but to keep her on her course."

The church was not designed to be a reservoir, ever-receiving and retaining for itself God's spiritual blessings, but rather a conduit, conveying God's blessings on and out to others everywhere.

The holiest moment of the church service is the moment when God's people—strengthened by preaching—go out the door into the world to be the church.

3

HOW HEALTHY IS THE CHURCH OUTREACH PROGRAM?

Ministry Is Knowing the...
NEWER FACES IN THE SUNDAY SCHOOL

Growing churches have many things in common.
The most common is that growing churches have direction.

Someone once said there are three things that cause people to change.
    (1) When they hurt enough they have to.
    (2) When they learn enough that they want to.
    (3) When they receive enough they are able to.

They are on a mission and their members tend to be excited about and supportive of the purpose of their church.
Numerical increase lies at the heart of God's will for His church because every number represents a person brought to the Lord.
They have learned that reliance upon a single means or entry point designed to usher people into a lasting relationship with Christ is insufficient.

They see salvation as the starting point but recognize discipleship and training as additional needs.

Whether one agrees with every method used by a church is entirely left to the judgment of its reader. However, after much research over the last 30 years I can carefully state that the following things exist in growing churches. Most do not do all of the programs listed but somewhere each use some and learned where they can grow best and reach the most in their location who have joined them.

High on the list of growing churches is Teacher Training. They convert and teach people who believe as they do.

Second, there is a strong emphasis on the Word of God.

Third, evangelism is the heartbeat of every program. It is the fuel that fills the classrooms, training sessions, and church membership.

Fourth, they believe in order to fulfill the great commission that every person is seen as a mandate from God to reach everyone available. They do not see numbers as their main goal. They see the salvation of every individual as their only goal.

Lastly, growing churches believe in strong discipleship training. Just reaching a person for Christ is not completed until they are grounded in the Word of God and enabled to reach another themselves.

Many church growth specialists see the role of Sunday school as the greatest method in evangelizing for the church. They see the Great Commission as
(1) Going (Evangelizing),
(2) Baptizing (Assimilation),
(3) Teaching obedience (Discipling).

One thing for sure is that churches that are now growing have taken a look at what they were doing and have put their focus on outreach. If fact, nearly 50% of a growing church budget is directed toward growth and outreach.

Many growing churches use the following programs. While this is not a complete list, it is a compilation of things used by churches that have planned to grow.

Growing churches know their potentials within an area. They have studied who to reach and how to do so. They have a plan and they are working their plan. They took time to look around them and prayed to the Lord for the right way to reach them.

They have identified the age groups in their area. They have learned that the needs of each vary and each have different value systems. While there is sometimes a struggle for the church that is expanding they have dedicated themselves so sincerely to reaching people for Christ that prayer and relationships have become paramount in their decision making.

You will find following the list of **NEWER FACES IN THE SUNDAY SCHOOL** which I put together in an acrostic format sharing the things that growing churches recognize as important to them.

N   NURSERY

A great amount of emphasis is placed on clean nurseries. One researcher said that the Millennial's, Generation X's and Bridger's age groups (which are the largest child baring age groups) would more likely return to a church because of the cleanliness of the nursery workers rather than denominational name or doctrine of the church.

E   EVANGELISTIC

Growing churches have people that totally believe that those without Christ are lost unless they reach them. They know they make a difference. They have learned the following facts about assimilation and the changes over the last 40 years.

(1) They know that 60% of those visiting their church come with little or no understanding of the church doctrine. While 40 years ago 90% rejoined a church of their denomination.

(2) There are 50% less people coming in the car today than the 4.2 in a car forty years ago.

(3) That today churches lose about 10% of their worshipers each year compared to 5% four decades ago.

(4) A church must keep 16% of its first time guests to grow 5% yearly. To grow 50 new members' means you will need to have 300 guests attend this year.

(5) That growing churches keep 85% of first-time visitor-if they attend two Sundays consecutively. They are aware that friendliness and the potential for growth are the two key factors for the guests return.

(6) Those who become active in church do so within Twelve months of their first attending.

(7) Newcomers must have at least 7 friends within six months of their first attendance.

W   WORSHIP STYLE

Most growing churches have a simple, less formal style of worship. Their services are warm and friendly.

E   ENROLLMENT

One of the great outreaches done by churches growing though their Sunday schools is that of enrolling people in the market places for Bible studies in their church. Sunday school Bible studies can be one of the best ways to reach the unsaved. Most church growth researchers have learned that new people are hard to assimilate into classes over two years old. This reveals that classes at that age and beyond are closed to the outsider. Therefore, churches who are growing with new people start new classes every two years which include 20% of their new people. They have learned that most classes older than two years are not growing. At least one of every five should have been started in the past two years. The reason: new groups grow more quickly. Churches do this at each year as they promote their students.

R   RELATIONSHIPS

These churches have learned that all needs are built around met needs. Therefore, they place a lot of importance on building new friendships. Newcomers enter a church looking for 3 key elements of life:

(1) Friends,
(2) A place to belong
(3) Ministry.

New classes generally can develop loving friendships, group identity and a place for service. One interesting research showed the value of friendship evangelism. It revealed that 85% of people led to the Lord by a friend stay in church, while 77% of those who drop out of church were led to the Lord by a stranger.

F   FAMILY

Great churches are aware of the changes in family units. They are aware that in 2010 half of the American population were single. That divorce is increasing yearly and the knowledge that half of all adults under 30 will lived with a partner before marriage. They are attempting to meet the multiple family that numbers more than 35 million step-parents. Their heart goes out to the 10% of all under age 18 that live with a step or single parent.

A   ADULTS

There are 254 million adults in the U.S., so programs are being created to reach the entire family by reaching the adults. One of the new frontiers for the church is the 20-35 age which is the most unreached group in America. However, while atheism and secularism is strong in this age many are returning to church for answers that education or wealth has not given them. Of the older church crowd it is estimated that one of seven have multiple church homes and that loyalty is less than 40 years ago.

C   CURRICULUM

One should be aware that all publishers have an agenda and theological positions. There are at least four main types of curriculum philosophies promoted by Sunday school publishers:

The Uniform lesson concept is usually those that design their courses by using the International lesson series. These publishers pay a 3% royalty to the National Council of Churches and will only cover about 30% of the Bible before they recycle the age groups.

The Unified lesson concept lends more to a topical approach. Most publishers using this method cover about 40% of the Bible in the adult age and many use the International Lesson series in some of their courses.

The Departmental lesson concept is more like the school systems approach which begins with where the previous age group stopped. They add to knowledge already known for each level. This is the lesson plan used by most churches, both small and large, because it represents the best educational and spiritual curriculum plan available. This is the Christian education philosophy used by Randall House Publications. Those who follow this concept will cover the complete Bible in the adult cycle and give broad ranges to those age groups from high school down.

The Closely graded concept is used mainly by the large church because there is a course for every age from grade 1 to grade 12. They use the Departmental concept in the preschool age group and College through senior adults.

Most churches and publisher will grade their Sunday school program as follows: Cradle, age 0-2; Nursery age 3-4; Preschool age 5-6; Primary grade 1 to 3; Junior grade 4-6; Junior High grade 7-9; High school grade 10-12; Adults from college to at least three levels of adulthood and the larger churches.

E   ELECTIVES

Along with regular curriculum most churches are adding extra courses of study either in regular class periods or in small groups outside the church building. The studies range from courses on the Family or Home, a special book subject but always there are classes of training because they know with their growth will come the need to train teachers. The growing church knows that for every one trained worker they can expect ten additional people. As an example, if you have 5 teachers you probably have around 50 in Sunday school. If 10 you will be running about 100, etc.

Therefore, growing churches have Teacher training programs designed to expand their growth.

Today more people are menu driven and want a selection of items to choose from. This has moved into the church as well and especially in the 20-35 age group.

S   SEEKER CLASSES

The seeker concept is not a new idea. It actually was very strong in the time of D.L. Moody and could have been the reason for much of his success as a revivalist. The church of his day was closed to outsiders and had nearly isolated themselves from doing the work design by the Lord. However, many people were searching for answers to their spiritual needs and were drawn by mass evangelism because it was an unthreatened place people could go to be saved. Church historians and growth researchers compare that era with our time. They mutually agree that our time is nearly the same as that period because they view the church today as closed to outsiders with assimilation being one of the churches greatest problems.

Many fundamental churches have seen the failure of their outreach programs and have begun to target the needs of their area or targeted age groups in their community. A number of years ago when I was president of a publishing company, a pastor asked us to print 18,000 eight page full color brochures entitled, "How to Handle Stress Before It Handles You." Welcome to our eight sermons that will help you with your problems was the thrush of the beautiful booklet. His area was surveyed he learned that his demographic age had a 35 year old average. He was aware that by this age's admission that they are the most stressed age group in our society. Whether this is true or not is not the issue. They think they are so. He was offering a solution and help. The end result is to reach them for Christ.

This method can reach far more than a year of Thursday night visitations. And think of the excitement of many new families coming to the Lord and being genuinely saved.

In essence the church strategy is to reach those who are seeking answers and investigating Christianity. And this will become more a need since most of the newcomers to our country are from non-Christian nations. Also, as our own nationality wanes, many of our newer members and visitors will know little about the Bible.

I   IMAGE

Churches that are on the move have a concern about how they look and if they are easy to find. But their greatest concern is their image in the community. How they are perceived by their neighborhood or city. Are we known as a soul-winning Bible-believing church or a fighting one? Some churches have relocated and changed their name to erase the poor image in their area. Researchers say it is not the name of the church nor the denominational name that matters as much as the vision of the pastor and its program. Great churches know the program gets people to the church but the pastor and his outlook keeps them.

N   NEW CONVERT - MEMBERSHIP CLASSES

Because most church members don't know the doctrine of the church or why the church exists, today's growing church teaches these subjects because they know it is the glue that bonds the church fellowship.

T   TEACHER TRAINING INSTITUTES

Most growing churches have Bible Institute Training programs going on at times other than Sunday services. Healthy growing churches know they can draw from at least 50% of their adult age for additional training. They learned that informed and trained people are more excited and stay longer. Example of courses: Teacher training, Doctrine, Christian Living, Soul-winning and Parenting are just a few a church can teach. Bible Institutes can be held in the spring and the fall with at least 12 nights in each season for class study. Be sure to issue a certificate of completion or require so many course completions before the larger or main diploma.

H   HANDICAP

There are more than 35 million who are Deaf, Retarded, Disabled, and Shut-in in the United States. Some of these handicapped will need people with an extra training. This portion of our society is twice the amount of teens in America. They need the gospel as others and have not been overlooked by the growing church.

E   ETHNIC CHANGES

Multiple congregations exist in many of Americas growing churches. The American society has seen more changes in the last decade than since the U. S. began a few hundred years ago. Today our society is composed of more than 500 ethnic groups and our demographic sources reveal 495 known American Indian tribes. In 2010 the census revealed that 636 languages are spoken in the U.S. The last 10 years have seen changes in the minorities that will affect the church.

In the area of birth increases during the last decade, there has been a Zero birth change in the Anglo-American community. That means those born with ancestors in Europe are not growing in our country. The reason is that while the last 100 years 83% of our country came from Europe, but today 75% of our immigrants come from the Pacific Rim of Asia descent and Latin America. A difference this makes to the church and our society is that our newest citizens come from non-Christian countries with a non-Biblical religion.

The black community is showing only a 2% birth increase. There are more blacks in America than any place else other than Nigeria. In 2012 US Census Bureau estimated 44,456,009 African

Americans in the United States meaning that 14.1% of the total American population of 313.9 Million is Black. Only about 30% of the black community has been touched by the church while 50% of black Africa knows Christ.

The Hispanic community has shown an 11% birth increase during this same time and represent about 35% of our present immigration. In October of the year 2000 they became larger that the black society and became the largest minority in the United States with 50,477,594 a 43% increase from 2000.The movement reaching the most Hispanic is the U.S. are the Mormon Church. Only about 3% of the Spanish community is evangelical.

But put on your seat belts! The Asian American community is growing at a faster pace than any race of our society. Their birth increase stands at about 18% and they represent nearly 65% of the immigration quota which now stands at 700,000 yearly. In 2050 they will pass the Hispanic people as the largest minority. This society will be different that most other minority groups. All of which will offer a challenge to the church and government. The Asian-American are better educated than any other society in this country. Forty-four percent of them have B.A. degrees as compared to the 25% of the rest of our population. Another difference is they bring religions that are not Bible based. Ancestor worship, Buddhism, Hinduism and many other unfamiliar religions will flood our nation. The American church will become as challenged as our missionaries that have gone to the foreign countries. Growing churches have looked beyond the skin of a person or his country of origin and are truly fulfilling the great commission of our Lord. Only one of the oriental groups that has had a Christian influence is Korea. Koreans in America are friendly toward churches with an open door. We can be a foreign missionary right here in the United States.

As the Asia community surfaces as the largest minority group the Angelo-American community will become an official minority. We are becoming a society run by four minority groups.

S   SINGLES CLASSES

The singles growth factor is one of the faster growing ministries in expanding churches. They know that this part of our society now represents 50% of our country. The never married or the single again is a targeted group by these churches.

U   USHERS/GREETERS

One of the most important roles in a church pledged to growth is the one who greets new people as they visit the church for the first time. They see the church like him and his personality. Growing churches choose friendly and cordial people to man the entrances to their church. They train these to give direction and keep order. Likewise, these churches do not use the term visitor. They have learned that the word visitor alienates. The word guest comes closest to what an outsider desires to be called because it places the feeling of one honored. Another thing known today is that a guest will probably not fill out your card because he knows the reason for it. He wants to make the selection himself to come to your church without pressure. Enlightened outreach leaders in growing churches have developed other ways to get the names and addresses and have used the friendship method to channel them to the church and Lord Jesus.

N   NURTURE

Because the growth of some churches have been greater than they prepared have designed compact disks, books, correspondence courses, videos, library, and Tudors to help those who want to learn more than the church staff can give. These are but a few things growing churches are doing to nurture.

D   DISCIPLESHIP

Always in the agenda of the growing church is the discipleship of the newer converts or transfers. Within these local churches are programs designed to teach or train. It is never finished because these outreaching churches are always bringing in new ones to be disciples.

A   AGING

The over aged 65 have outnumbered teens since December of 1983. One half of all people who have lived beyond 65 live now. Nearly 12 percent of the American population is over age 65. Twenty percent of those in this age group attend church. Also, the over 65 is multiplying three times faster than the rest of the population. In 2010, One fourth of all Americans were over 65. In the same year one of four will have children who are 65 also.

Vision looks inward and becomes a **Duty.**

Vision look outward and becomes **Aspiration**

Vision looks upward and becomes **Faith**

Y   YOUTH

Today there are 22 million teens in the U.S. The social problems of the last three decades have contributed too many of the ills of this age group. Ten percent of all teens under the age of 18 have grown up with a single step-parent.

Statistics reveal an alarming future for many of our teens. Children of divorced parents are more likely themselves to:
1. Divorce.
2. Never be saved.
3. Go to jail.
4. Not believe in God,
5. Not get a high paying job.

6. Not finish school.
7. Not own a home.
8. Not get permanent job until mid-20.
9. Not to get married.
10. Not go to college.
11. Not be involved in ministry, and
12. More likely to give spousal abuse.

S   SMALL GROUPS

There are nearly as many small group studies outside the church as Sunday school classes. The growing church has connected these to their educational program and used them as feeders to their church.

C   COMMUNITY CONSCIOUS

The growing church is becoming a flagship in the affairs of the community. It helps to set the direction of its social order. It is heard as its leadership affects the affairs of the community. Many churches have begun to reenter the schools with Bible Clubs, Child Evangelism Fellowship, helping the lower income children and inviting them to Upward Basketball and Awana program.

H   HOMOGENEITY

The growing church targets those that are of same types and kinds. They know they are not able to reach everyone, so plan for those most likely to jell with the churches program.

O   OUTREACH

The outreach of growing congregations are planned. They have learned that certain areas of society are reachable and concentrate on the ten most receptive groups of people to reach.

1. Second-time visitors to their church.
2. Close friends and relatives of new converts.
3. People going through a divorce.

4. Those who feel their need for a recovery program (alcohol, drugs, sexual, etc.).
5. First-time parents.
6. The terminal ill and their families.
7. Couples with major marriage problems.
8. Parents with problem children.
9. Recently unemployed or those with major financial problems.
10. New residents in the community.

O   ORGANIZATION

Growing churches plan to grow. They use mottoes, slogans, and banners to keep it ever before the people. They call people to prayer and training. They have learned not everyone will catch the spirit so lead those that rally behind the leadership of the church.

Nothing breeds excitement more than "We are growing." Somewhere before this statement they learned that "Vision looks inward and becomes a duty. Vision look outward and becomes aspiration. Vision looks upward and becomes faith." But they see the barriers and problems to organizational units.

- They know that 5% of their organization is made up by <u>self-starters</u> with confidence to do the job. These are the VIP's. All they need is the affirmation of the leader. Time on the leader to keep them going is only about 5%.
- Every student of organizational structure know that about 15% of its people are trainable. VTP's are the <u>Very Trainable People</u>. These are the available ones willing to learn and be used. They take up about 20% of the leader's time. (About 95% of all people who become active in the organization were introduced to it by these first

two groups.)

- The third group in an organization are the VNP's. The <u>Very Nice People</u>. They make up 75% of a church or organization. They are nice, friendly, and the type that give you extras, cause you no problems, but do not come back of Sunday or Wednesday nights and you cannot count on them for leadership or dedication to roles or tasks in the organization. The good thing is they only take about 25% of the leader's time.

- There is however a group called the VDP's that represent 5% of the church or organization but demand 50% of the leader's time. These are the <u>Very Demanding People.</u> They never visit, most don't support the church or program of the church, but are always draining the leader's time and keeping the organization from fulfilling its reason for existence.

Most leaders of growing churches or organization have learned than they had to finally conclude that for them to grow it meant going with those who shared his vision and wanted to help rather than hurt the leaders goal. Successful pastors that are growing have elected officers that have a Great commission conscience. Growing churches expect their members to be Great Commission thinkers. Another factor in Sunday school growth discovered by growing churches called the Role/Task Ratio.

There should be at least 60 roles and tasks available for every 100 members in the church. When one counts the Deacons, Trustees, officers of the church he is still short. But if you have a Class President, Vice-president, secretary, treasurer, outreach people in your Sunday school and Training departments you create roles in which a person can function thus exceeding the amount needed.

L   LEADERSHIP

No pastor has ever built beyond his desire or leadership. While many large churches have pastors that are not excellent pulpit men, they are filled with men of vision and who are able to get the ear and heart of his followers. He has shown them the way and they trust him and his leadership to get them to the goal or dream. This type of leader knows he cannot do it all himself so builds leaders under him that common goal. He shares his dream and teaches the mandate of Jesus Christ. No church has ever grown much until the membership totally believes that everyone in their community and world is lost until they have won them to Christ and their church.

Growing churches have pastors that look beyond just the preaching service. He sees the training and teaching program of his church as high on his list of priorities. He seeks those that share his convictions and places them in roles that complement the growth program. Churches know the POLE method. Plan. Organize. Lead. Evaluate.

S   SUPERINTENDENT

The pastor-leader that moves his church beyond its earlier status nearly always had a Sunday school Director of Christian Education or Superintendent that shared his conviction for growth. These two are both extremely convinced that the preaching and teaching program of the church are necessary for future enlargement. The Sunday school and educational agency is the Bible in "work clothes." Most churches have in place already the mechanism for the easiest and best way for church growth. It is the Sunday school that has every age group in place, is the teaching arm of the church, and could be organized to reach more quickly than any program ever invented.

While some of these programs are not new, they are being used today for church growth.

4

Does The Health Of Your Church Come From Change?

Ministry Is Seeing ...
CHANGE

I have some level of enjoyment looking at old predictions. Those thoughts from the past seemed very informed at the time of their predictions. The church has seen more changes in the past three decades than the previous eight decades combined. Who would then be so audacious to foretell for the church? Such is the risk I take in writing this article.

Please understand that I make these predictions with less audacity than it might appear on the surface. Tom Rainer and his research team and studied more than 4,000 churches and interviewed thousands of church leaders, church members, and unchurched persons. I do not have a crystal ball or some prophetic abilities. The trends you are about to read are based on current developments, for which I have simply extrapolated to the future.

Their order is random, and does not reflect some type of priority or certainty of expectation. So buckle your seatbelt and let us delve into the next few years of church life.

1.   The increasing interest in spiritual warfare. The wildly popular Left Behind book series is only symptomatic of the increasing interest in the world of spiritual warfare. And after the many pronouncements of the reality and presence of evil after Sept. 11, people across America are seeking answers in a world where evil is a real and present reality.

How will church leaders respond? There will naturally be the extremes present in any movement. On the one hand, some churches will continue to ignore the reality of the demonic world as if Ephesians 6 has little to do with their day-by-day existence. On the other hand, there will be churches that see demonic activity in every phase of the church life.

It was always a scary thing to me as a lad growing up when I would hear of these unusual stories from missionaries from South and Central America. The stories of demons finally came to a reality to me when visiting in Brazil a few years back. After a long hard day, I excused myself from the missionaries in whose home I was a guest and prepared for a night of rest. After a brief look at the Bible and a very short prayer, I soon found myself in a deep sleep. In the middle of the night, I heard a voice that appeared to be saying to me. "I want to enter your body." I awoke and thought perhaps I had been in a bad dream so I returned back to sleep and the same voice repeated the same saying to me. At this time I immediately fell to my knees beside the bed and now my prayer was not a little sweet one. I sincerely said, in the name of Jesus depart from me! The next morning the missionaries at the breakfast table said I heard your sincere prayer last night at which time I responded with what I just recorded here in. This was my first experience with a demonic atmosphere and they explained to me that it was definitely real in their city in Brazil.

Church members must be taught the biblical balance of the supernatural world. Church leaders must also be taught the biblical percepts of spiritual warfare. In a survey of 23 seminaries, only seven taught any courses related to spiritual warfare, but of those seven, leaders in those seminaries indicated that the courses were among the most popular.

The closing of 50,000 churches by 2015. Thousands of churches are on the precipice of closing. The conventional wisdom was that churches were tenaciously stubborn, and could keep going for years. But those churches were led by the builder generation, those born before 1946. The church going builders attended churches out of loyalty and tradition. They would often remain loyal to a church despite deteriorating quality and attendance.

But boomers, busters/Gen Xer's, and Bridger's - those born between 1977 and 1994 - have no such loyalties. They see no need to remain with a church that exists out of tradition and with little care for the quality of the ministries. Though I am not happy to report this trend, the fading of the builder generation indicates the death of one out of eight churches in America today.

2. A research done by the Southern Baptist convention showed a surge in the number of churches whose attendance is below 300. A trend that may somewhat offset the loss of churches will be the starting of new churches with a planned attendance cap. In other words, from the point of birth of these churches, the members will not let attendance move above a predetermined cap, most commonly in the 200 to 300 range. When the attendance approaches the cap, the members will plan to start another church. Of course, the daughter church will have the same ministry, so the number of these smaller churches will continue to grow with the same philosophy of size. Why will these churches proliferate? Both Gen X and the Bridger generation include millions of young adults who desire the small church intimacy of 300 or less. But they have been unable to find many small churches that offer quality preaching, child care, youth programs, and the like. Therefore, they will start their own churches with a focus on quality while remaining relatively small.

The incredible influence of the Bridger generation. The impact of those born between 1977 and 1994 will be more than just the starting of new churches mentioned in the previous trend. The paradoxical implication of this generation is that there are fewer Christians in this age range than previous generations, but their impact will be more profoundly felt than the larger numbers of Christians in the older age groups.

As few as 4 percent of the 72 million Bridger generation may have a born-again experience. Yet, that 4

The Disappearance of Doctrine

Forty years ago, 90% of churchgoers were faithful to a specific church or denomination because they believed in the doctrines taught by that church. Today 60% of those visiting a church come with little or no understanding of ANY church doctrine.

This problem is complicated by an American culture that has moved the Christian God out of its consciousness. The media portrays a culture devoid of any meaningful Christian content or practice.

On campuses and in the media, the only absolutes these days is that there are no absolutes. Morality is radically individual, as people decide what is right or wrong with no standard to go by but their own feelings and wishes.

Many live most of their days alone with a machine. Increasingly people prefer to communicate electronically because it is safer and very controlled. As a result, life is impersonal and often empty.

percent will practice a radical Christianity. They will take their faith more seriously than previous generations. And many will go into dangerous mission fields, willing to give their lives for the sake of the gospel.

The churches that make a difference will not do church the way the way it's always done. Since the church will no longer be a part of the mainstream culture, it cannot expect to survive or thrive with the loyal churchgoer base of old.

The Bridger generation will not be satisfied with business as usual in the churches. And those churches that desire to reach the second-largest generation in America's history better be prepared to give more than lip service to the cause of Christ. These young people are shaking life up in many churches.

The increasing demand for clarity and conviction in doctrine. Led by the Bridger generation and Gen X, those who come to the churches of the 21st century are increasingly seeking to learn the tenets of the Christian faith. They are not satisfied with coming to church for the sake of coming to church. They desire to know more of what they believe, and they insist that the church and her leaders express conviction about these beliefs. The churches that survive and grow in the years ahead will provide numerous opportunities for members and seekers to learn more about the faith to which they adhere.

The Implications

Few would argue that the Christian faith in America is slowly but perceptibly being moved to the margins of society. The churches that make a difference will not do church the way we've always done it. Since the church will no longer be a part of the mainstream culture, it cannot expect to survive or thrive with the loyal churchgoer base of old.

As you will see, these times are either the most exciting or the most disturbing for church leaders. You will see some of the most challenging days in the church in recent history. We serve a God through whom all things are possible. Let us go forward in the confidence of His strength and not our own.

In a recent conference on stock market trends, one of the speakers boldly declared that "one who predicts the future is either omniscient or a fool."

In the Southern Baptists research over the last nine years has examined more than 4,000 churches. They interviewed countless persons, both churched and unchurched, on their attitudes about the church. And have observed innumerable cultural trends that directly impact the church.

As we look at the trends for the church, a common thread runs through all of them. "Successful churches" are becoming high commitment and high expectation churches. For nearly 50 years, a majority of American churches eased into the ruts of routine and low expectations. One could be a "member in good standing" in some of the churches without attending church for an entire year! But the times are now changing indeed.

Stabilized church attendance with declining church membership. It is no easy task to measure church attendance in America. Even in a single church, measurement standards are often inconsistent or nonexistent. Many of the polls of recent years suggest that church attendance has been mostly stable for the past four decades.

The leveling of attendance must be seen as a positive development in light of a quarter of century of declining numbers. But church membership, largely stable for decades, is showing early signs of erosion. Is this trend healthy or unhealthy?

A better indicator of church involvement is attendance rather than membership. But the early indicators of declining membership may not be negative signs. Many church leaders, frustrated with nominal and nonexistent members, are purging their rolls. One large church recently removed 10,000 members from its rolls. Yet the attendance in the church has seen healthy increases. It would appear that the positive perspective of this trend is that more church leaders are taking church membership more seriously.

The emergence of "homegrown" ministers in 30 percent of all full-time ministry positions in the local church. Most followers of American church life would express surprise that an increasing number of churches are finding full-time ministry staff persons within the ranks of their own membership. A recent sampling found that 8 percent of all staff ministers were "home grown."

The number of such ministers has increased significantly in the past three years. The proportion has doubled from 4 percent to 8 percent just since 1999. Based upon these trends, it is anticipated that nearly one out of three full-time staff ministers in the local church will be called from the ranks of laypersons in that particular church.

The implications are many. One obvious benefit is that each of these ministers will have an intimate knowledge of the church. The minister will certainly believe in the core values and the church's vision. And training time will be minimal since an orientation to the church will not be needed.

But a possible concern is the lack of formal and theological training of the minister, seminary or otherwise. Some churches, realizing both the advantage of homegrown ministers and the disadvantage of their having no formal training, have partnered with seminaries to have the best of both worlds. Watch for this trend to grow in this decade.

An increase in intentional evangelistic ministries focused on children and youth. Research shows that 82 percent of American Christians became Christians before the age of 20. While this statistic is noteworthy, even more amazing is the number of Christians who accepted Christ before the age of 14 - 75 percent, according to research.

A casual observer would probably expect churches to be intensely involved in evangelistic activity, based on some awareness of the young people's receptivity. An additional impetus, it would seem, would be the large numbers of this generation. Most of them belong to the Bridger generation, the second largest generation in America's history. The young people born between 1977 and 1994 exceed 72 million.

But the reality is that relatively few churches are intensely intentional about evangelizing or pre-evangelizing children and youth. Most churches seem to ignore their own data, which shows, according to our research, vacation Bible school to be the most effective evangelistic tool used today. Most of the highly intentional evangelizing activity for young people has been led by para-church organizations.

We see a reversal in this trend. Early signs indicate a significant interest by local churches in reaching and evangelizing children and youth. Some of the most innovative new church buildings are for youth and children. Church leaders are examining closely the numbers of conversions of young people. And even more leaders are becoming increasingly aware of the competition for the souls of America's youth. Mormons, Jehovah's Witnesses, and Muslims, to name a few, have not been shy about proselytizing young people. Look for more churches to become highly intentional about reaching children and youth.

Americans Have Grown To Accustomed To Change.

An increasing number of churches with succession plans for their senior pastor or minister. An abundance of research has made clear the importance of the senior pastor or minister in a local church's health or growth. Yet most churches have no idea what will take place when their present pastor leaves.

In a survey of 312 churches, only seven had some type of plan in place when their pastor resigned, moved or died. We believe, however, that the trend will develop where more and more churches have some type of plan in place.

A few significant churches have established succession plans, and many other church leaders are observing closely. Southeast Christian Church in Louisville, Ky., one of America's largest churches, has a clearly established succession plan in place. When senior minister Bob Russell retired, associate minister Dave Stone was in place to take the leadership helm.

This trend is beginning to take root in some mid-size churches with attendance of 300 to 700. Researchers believe the number will grow.

The emergence of a children's minister as the third full-time staff minister. Researchers are frequently asked the "best" priority for calling and hiring staff ministers. Which position, after pastor, should be our second staff person? Should that person be full-time or part-time? Which position is next? The questions seem endless.

The traditional hiring pattern has been pastor, music/worship, and then numerous possibilities for the third. The third position may include education, discipleship, missions, administration, youth or student. The context and needs of the church, as well as past patterns, typically determine the choice.

Sunday school is Changing in Under-the-Radar But Significant Ways. Certainly all methods of ministry need to be evaluated constantly with regard to their effectiveness and how they fit into God's purpose for the church.

For many American churches the focus has been almost exclusively on converting people to a code of Christian conduct with the hope that they will 'behave' their way to salvation.

I grew up with Sunday school. I found that I had a solid foundation of Biblical education to instruct me in the new way of life I had followed.

It's easy to demolish a structure, not so easy to replace it with a new one. Simply renaming Sunday school as "Discipleship Hour" is not much of an advance. The Sunday schools that I experienced were that already. Perhaps a name change is helpful so that this ministry will not be regarded merely as a relic from the past, but simply changing the name doesn't mean much unless there is a fresh vision from God.

Americans have grown accustomed to change. But children who attend Sunday school these days have an experience similar to that which their grandparents would have had decades ago. In a culture saturated with change, one of the most stable aspects in the religious sphere has been Sunday school – the weekend educational efforts that Protestant churches offer to people outside of worship services.

However, a new study conducted by The Barna Group of Ventura, California shows that while many aspects of Sunday school remain constant, there are significant changes bubbling beneath the surface. Longitudinal research among Protestant pastors, commissioned by Gospel Light, has explored how churches prioritize and engage in Sunday school, the usage of curriculum, midweek programming for children, and Vacation Bible School programs (often called VBS).

Things Stay the Same...And Things Change

Church reliance upon Sunday school has remained stable: 19 out of every 20 Protestant churches (95%) offer a Sunday school in which people receive some form of planned or systematic Bible instruction in a class setting. Nearly the same proportion of churches – 97% – offered Sunday school eight years ago, when the tracking research began, while churches are often divided along denominational, theological, and methodological lines, the research points out that Sunday school remains one of the most widely embraced ministry programs.

However, the fact that so many churches offer Sunday school may mask some of the changes taking place. The research identified three changes shaping up within Sunday school programs – and two additional shifts affecting other children's programs. Those alterations related to Sunday school include a declining percentage of pastors who claim that Sunday school is their top priority; fewer churches offering Sunday school for children under age six or for junior-high or high-school students; and the increased customization of curriculum by churches. The other two changes affecting children's ministry include a drop in the number of churches offering a VBS program and a decline in the prevalence of midweek programming for children.

A Declining Priority

In terms of Sunday school prioritization, the research showed that just 1 in every 7 Senior Pastors (15%) considers Sunday school to be their church's highest priority. This represents a significant drop from previous years – 2002 was the high point, when 22% of pastors claimed that Sunday school was the top priority of their church.

What types of pastors were least likely to prioritize Sunday school? Those leading mainline churches (8%), pastors under 40 years of age (10%), and predominately white congregations (12%). On the other hand, those most likely to strongly emphasize Sunday school were African-American congregations (37%), Baptist churches (23%), pastors who have been leading their churches for 20 or more years (23%), charismatic churches (21%), and congregations with pastors age 59 or older (21%).

Cutting Out Those on the Edges

Another significant change is that fewer churches are offering Sunday school programs for the youngest and oldest children – including adolescents and teenagers. Churches are less likely to offer programming for children under the age of two, dropping six percentage points since 1997 (79% to 73%). They were also less likely to offer Sunday school programs for children ages two to five (declining 94% to 88%), as well as for junior high (dropping from 93% to 86%) and high school students (moving from 86% to 80%). These may not seem like substantial drops in terms of percentage points – after all, a large majority of churches continues to offer such programs – but, it represents about 20,000 fewer churches providing Sunday school for each age group.

One of the signs pointing to additional changes in the future is that pastors with the shortest tenure in ministry (one to five years) were less likely than more experienced pastors to offer five out of the six types of Sunday school programming (the only exception being junior high classes). While a majority of these young pastors continue to offer Sunday school, they are at the leading edge of experimenting without traditional Sunday school.

The most common Sunday school programming is offered for elementary age children (grades 1 through 6) and for adults. Currently, more than 9 out of every 10 churches offer Sunday school for elementary grades (92%) and adults (91%). These levels are statistically unchanged since 1997.

Customizing the Content

The fastest-moving shift within Sunday school programming is the move toward "customized" curriculum. Currently, 1 out of every 5 churches (18%) creates their own curriculum for elementary-age classes – nearly double the percentage measured in 2002 (10%).

The profile of churches most likely to create their own curriculum is revealing. The data show that Buster pastors (26%) and those in the West (25%) – often viewed as pace-setters for other regions – are among the most likely to customize, suggesting that the trend is likely to grow in prominence. The churches least likely to customize were Southern Baptist (4%) and African American (9%). Although the research did not define "customization" for pastors, the interviews suggest it ranges from simplistic efforts (e.g., piecing together lesson plans and coloring pages from previous years) to investing significant staff time and creative energy into crafting a complete curriculum from scratch.

Still, the most common type of elementary-aged Sunday school curriculum used among churches is that produced by their denomination. In total, 52% of all pastors report purchasing this type of curriculum. One in every four pastors (26%) indicated that their church buys curriculum from an independent publisher.

Other Programs

Another shift in children's ministry has been the 15% decline in the percentage of churches offering Vacation Bible School (or VBS) – from 81% to 69%. That represents about 38,000 fewer churches offering VBS than a few years ago. Those most likely to offer VBS were Southern Baptist and mainline churches, congregations with 250 or more adult attenders, and black congregations. Among those least likely to have VBS were charismatic or Pentecostal congregations, churches in the West, churches attracting fewer than 100 adult attenders, and churches whose pastor has been serving in full-time ministry for less than six years.

Why not offer VBS? A lack of teachers is still the most common reason (mentioned by 23% of pastors). Interestingly, pastors are becoming increasingly likely to mention that their church has "no time" for VBS (up from 5% in 2001 to 13% now) or that they "offer other activities" (up from less than 1% to 12% now).

The fifth shift identified by the Barna study was a 10% drop in the proportion of churches that have midweek programming for kids (slipping from 64% to 58% in study). This represents a drop of nearly 20,000 churches. Midweek programming was most common among Southern Baptists, large churches, churches in the South and Midwest, and charismatic congregations, and least common among mainline churches, small churches, and those located in the West or Northeast. Pastors who have been at their current church for more than a decade were also more likely than were short-tenured pastors to offer midweek programming.

Perspective on the Changes

Anticipating that some people will infer that Sunday school is fading, David Kinnaman, the director of the study, explained that, "rumors of Sunday school's imminent demise are greatly exaggerated. Every weekend more than 300,000 churches offer some type of systematic religious instruction in a classroom setting – and those programs are attended by nearly 45 million adults and more than 22 million youth and children. In fact, nearly 9 out of every 10 pastors said they consider Sunday school to be an important part of their church's ministry. The changes facing Sunday school seem to be more about the form – not the function – of Sunday school. It appears as though churches are moving toward a 'label-less' future: they will offer summertime programs, but not necessarily VBS, and they will continue to prioritize Christian education, but not necessarily Sunday school."

The Barna Group's Vice President continued: "The most significant part of the changing landscape, however, is the new identity being carved out by Buster pastors and those relatively new in ministry. Where these young leaders will take Sunday school and VBS is anyone's guess. Although many Buster pastors currently deploy Sunday school programs, they seem open to new methods and approaches and less driven by tradition or program loyalty. Many Buster pastors possess a means-to-an-end perspective about Sunday school and VBS, which suggests the churches they lead will be more apt to adopt innovations in spiritual training."

"When it comes to ministry to children specifically, pastors are facing a bevy of pressures and demands that have precipitated many of these changes," commented Kinnaman. "Many pastors are coming to realize that ministry to children must be one of – if not the – preeminent emphases of their church. Ministry to children is highly strategic. Young people are spiritual sponges whose most impressionable years are too important to pass up. In contrast, changing adults' spiritual perspectives is a hit-or-miss proposition. Further, churches face increasingly complex demands to partner with and equip parents. There are pressures that Sunday school provide one-of-a-kind experiences and facilitate clearer and deeper outcomes in the lives of children. There are also increased expectations placed on churches for personal choice and for multimedia relevance. Without compromising the Gospel, Sunday school and other forms of Christian education must continue to adapt to be effective in this ever-changing environment."

Research Methodology

In this report, "small churches" were defined as those that attract less than 100 adults to their weekend events on a typical weekend. "Mid-sized churches" in this study were those that attract 100 to 250 adults; large churches were those attracting 250 or more adults.

Let me also address another age group that the church and Sunday school are endeavoring to keep in the church. They are commonly referred to as Millennials or Bridger's those born between 1984 and 2002.

Reasons Millennials Stay Connected to Church

A controversial topic was reignited when blogger and author Rachel Held Evans wrote a piece about why Millennials leave church. Her editorial struck a nerve, sparking response pieces all across the web and generating more than 100,000 social media reactions in the first week alone.

The relationship between Millennials and the Church is shifting.

Yet whatever one's personal view of the reasons behind Millennials staying or going, one thing is clear: the relationship between Millennials and the Church is shifting. Barna Group's researchers have been examining Millennials' faith development since the generation was in its teen years—that is, for about a decade. During that time, the firm has conducted 27,140 interviews with members of the millennial generation in more than 200 studies.

And while Barna Group's research has previously highlighted what's not working to keep Millennials at church, the research also illuminates what is working—and what churches can do to engage these young adults.

The Harsh Realities of Millennial Faith

But first, the concerns of Millennials leaving the Church must be understood.

Parents and leaders have long been concerned about the faith development of the generation born between 1984 and 2002—and for good reason. First, Barna research shows nearly six in ten (59%) of these young people who grow up in Christian churches end up walking away from either their faith or from the institutional church at some point in their first decade of adult life. Second, the unchurched segment among Millennials has increased in the last decade, from 44% to 52%, mirroring a larger cultural trend away from churchgoing among the nation's population.

Third, when asked what has helped their faith grow, "church" does not make even the top 10 factors. Instead, the most common drivers of spiritual growth, as identified by Millennials themselves, are prayer, family and friends, the Bible, having children, and their relationship with Jesus

Culture: Acceleration and Complexity

Still, not all is doom and gloom when it comes to faith among Millennials. In contrast to the widespread religious disillusionment marked among so many of their peers, millions of Christian Millennials remain deeply committed and active in their faith.

About one-quarter of 18- to 29-year-olds are practicing Christians, meaning they attend church at least once a month and strongly affirm that their religious faith is very important in their life. A majority of Millennials claim to pray each week, one-quarter say they've read the Bible or attended a religious small group this week, and one in seven have volunteered at a church in the past seven days.

These spiritual practices are notable, says David Kinnaman, president of Barna Group, because the broader cultural trends have not been particularly friendly to faith.

"Millennials are rethinking most of the institutions that arbitrate life, from marriage and media, to government and church," says Kinnaman, the author of *You Lost Me* and *Un-Christian* who has spent the last 20 months speaking nationally about the challenges facing today's Millennials. "They have grown up in a culture and among peers who are often neutral or resistant to the gospel. And life feels accelerated compared with 15 years ago—the ubiquity of information makes it harder for many to find meaning in institutions that feel out of step with the times. Millennials often describe church, for instance, as 'not relevant' or say that attending worship services 'feels like a boring duty.'

"Furthermore, many young Americans say life seems complicated—that it's hard to know how to live with the onslaught of information, worldviews and options they are faced with every day. One of the specific criticisms young adults frequently make about Christianity is that it does not offer deep, thoughtful or challenging answers to life in a complex culture."

But this criticism is also a sign of hope, Kinnaman suggests, since it means Millennials are craving depth—a need the Church is uniquely poised to meet. In this respect, the research points to five ways faith communities can build deeper, more lasting connections with Millennials.

Make room for meaningful relationships.

The first factor that will engage Millennials at church is as simple as it is integral: relationships. When comparing twentysomethings who remained active in their faith beyond high school and twentysomethings who dropped out of church, the Barna study uncovered a significant difference between the two. Those who stay were twice as likely to have a close personal friendship with an adult inside the church (59% of those who stayed report such a friendship versus 31% among those who are no longer active). The same pattern is evident among more intentional relationships such as mentoring—28% of Millennials who stay had an adult mentor at the church other than their pastor, compared to 11% of dropouts who say the same.

Kinnaman is quick to point out the limitations of such a study: "It's important for anyone who uses research to realize correlation does not equal causation.

"Yet, among those who remain active, this much is clear: the most positive church experiences among Millennials are relational. This stands true from the inverse angle as well: Seven out of 10 Millennials who dropped out of church did not have a close friendship with an adult and nearly nine out of ten never had a mentor at the church.

"The implication is that huge proportions of churchgoing teenagers do not feel relationally accepted in church. This kind of information should be a wake-up call to ministry leaders as well as to churched adults of the necessity of becoming friends with the next generation of believers Grace.

Teach Cultural Discernment.

A second important ministry outcome for today's Millennials is helping them develop discernment skills—especially in understanding and interpreting today's culture. For example, active Millennial Christians are more than twice as likely to say they "learned about how Christians can positively contribute to society" compared to those who drop out (46% versus 20%). Actives are also nearly four times more likely to say they "better understand my purpose in life through church" (45% versus 12%).

For a generation that already laments the complexity of modern life, the Church can offer valuable clarity. Millennials need help learning how to apply their hearts and minds to today's cultural realities. In many ways, pop culture has become the driver of religion for Millennials, so helping them think and respond rightly to culture should be a priority.

Although, such development must also take care to avoid the overprotective impulses that are driven by fear of culture. Rather, Millennials need guidance on engaging culture meaningfully, and from a distinctly Christian perspective. This idea of finding a way to bring their faith in Jesus to the problems they encounter in the world seems to be one of the most powerful motivations of today's practicing Christian Millennials. They don't want their faith to be relegated to Sunday worship, and this desire for holistic faith is something the Church can speak to in a meaningful way.

Make Reverse Mentoring A Priority.

A third thing Barna Group's team has learned about effective ministry to Millennials is that young people want to be taken seriously today—not for some distant future leadership position. In their eyes, institutional church life is too hierarchical. And they're not interested in earning their way to the top so much as they're want to put their gifts and skills to work for the local church in the present—not future—tense.

The term "reverse mentoring" has come to describe this kind of give and take between young and established leaders. Kinnaman says, "Effective ministry to Millennials means helping these young believers discover their own mission in the world, not merely asking them to wait their turn. One way to think about this generation is that they are exiles in something like a 'digital Babylon'—an immersive, interactive, image-rich environment in which many older believers feel foreign and lost. The truth is, the Church needs the next generation's help to navigate these digital terrains."

The research shows few churches help young people discover a sense of mission, though this too is important in cultivating a faith that lasts. Millennials who remain active in church are twice as likely as dropouts to say they served the poor through their church (33% versus 14%). They are also more likely to say they went on a trip that helped expand their thinking (29% versus 16%) and more likely to indicate they had found a cause or issue at church that motivates them (24% versus 10%).

Embrace the potency of vocational discipleship.

A fourth way churches can deepen their connection with Millennials is to teach a more potent theology of vocation, or calling. Millennials who have remained active are three times more likely than dropouts to say they learned to view their gifts and passions as part of God's calling (45% versus 17%). They are four times more likely to have learned at church "how the Bible applies to my field or career interests" (29% versus 7%). A similar gap exists when it came to receiving helpful input from a pastor about education (21% versus 5%), though going so far as offering a scholarship (5% versus 2%) was not particularly widespread.

"Most churches seem to leave this kind of vocation-based outcome largely at the door," comments Kinnaman, "unless these students show interest in traditional church-based ministry." But what Millennials are seeking goes beyond this. Kinnaman calls it "vocational discipleship," a way to help Millennials connect to the rich history of Christianity with their own unique work God has called them to.

Facilitate connection with Jesus.

Finally, more than a mere community club helping youth cross the threshold of adulthood, church communities can help Millennials generate a lasting faith by facilitating a deeper sense of intimacy with God. For example, Millennials who remain active are more likely than those who dropped out to say they believe Jesus speaks to them personally in a way that is real and relevant (68% versus 25%). Additionally, actives are much more likely to believe the Bible contains wisdom for living a meaningful life (65% versus 17%).

Millennials who retain a longer-lasting faith than their peers are more likely to find a sense of authority in the Word of God—both in the pages of the Bible as well as in their experience of intimacy with the God they follow.

"This means Millennials who retain a longer-lasting faith than their peers are more likely to find a sense of authority in the

Word of God—both in the pages of the Bible as well as in their experience of intimacy with the God they follow," Kinnaman says.

Of course, many church leaders are already trying to connect biblical authority to a personal relationship with Jesus for their young people. So what is happening to thwart these efforts?

Kinnaman explains, "In part, it is a failure of not connecting Jesus and the Bible to the other outcomes identified in this research—relational, missional, vocational and cultural discernment. In other words, the version of 'Jesus in a vacuum' that is often packaged for young people doesn't last long compared to faith in Christ that is not compartmentalized but wholly integrated into all areas of life."

A Handful of Caveats

There are several caveats that come with this kind of research, Kinnaman points out. "First, as Millennials are quick to say themselves, life is complicated—there are many significant influences at work in their lives today. These five principles are certainly not an exhaustive list, but it does reflect some of the things our team has learned so far.

"Second, parents as well as church and organizational leaders should be open to learning all they can about Millennials in order to maximize their efforts to spiritually engage them. However, they should take care not to idolize this emerging generation and in so doing create a form of age-ism. Millennials should be a priority not because 'youth must be served,' but because this generation is trying to learn faithfulness in a rapidly changing post-Christian culture. Millennials need the help of faithful believers from older generations if they are to make sense of it all and move meaningfully forward in their life and faith."

This is a necessary age if the future of the Sunday school and church continues. However, I am a realist and think you should know what you are facing.

What, if anything, helps Americans grow in their faith? When Barna Group asked, people offered a variety of answers—prayer, family or friends, reading the Bible, having children—but church did not even crack the top-10 list.

Although church involvement was once a cornerstone of American life, U.S. adults today are evenly divided on the importance of attending church. While half (49%) say it is "somewhat" or "very" important, the other 51% say it is "not too" or "not at all" important. The divide between the religiously active and those resistant to churchgoing impacts American culture, morality, politics and religion.

Looking to future generations does not paint an optimistic picture for the importance of churchgoing. Millennials (those 30 and under) stand out as least likely to value church attendance; only two in 10 believe it is important. And more than one-third of millennial young adults (35%) take an anti-church stance. In contrast, Elders (those over 68) are the most likely (40%) to view church attendance as "very" important, compared to one-quarter (24%) who deem it "not at all" important. Boomers (ages 49—67) and Gen Xers (ages 30—48) fall in the middle of these polar opposites. While the debate rages about what will happen to Millennials as they get older—Will they return to church attendance later in life?—they are starting at lower baseline for church participation and commitment than previous generations.

5

Having A Healthy Church May Come At Great Cost.

Ministry Is Knowing...
WHAT DOES IT COST TO GROW?

Second church averaged 205 in morning worship and on the surface appeared to be growing. Therefore, they voted 126 to 31 to attempt to double their church in 7 years. Because of the church building size the committee knew they would have to have 2 worship services to meet that goal. When this was voted on the decision was 98 to 62 rejecting to have two services.

I. THE MOST CRUCIAL IS THE ATTITUDE OF THE MEMBERS.
    A. *Distinction between following two factors:*
        1. *Wanting* to grow
        2. *Deciding* to grow
    B. *Know the enthusiasm level of the members.* A common characteristic of growing congregations is that members are enthusiastic about their faith as Christians; about the congregation of which they are members; and about the life, program, and ministry of that congregation.

1.   A high level of enthusiasm is a major price tag in church growth. Closely related to that *is the intensity of belief.* THE MEMBERS OF A GROWING CHURCH HAVE INTENSE CONVICTIONS ABOUT THEIR FAITH AND ABOUT THEIR CALL TO REACH THE UNCHURCHED.

2.   Another critical element in the attitudes of the people is that the MEMBERS RECOGNIZE THAT THEY DO HAVE CONSIDERABLE CONTROL OVER WHAT HAPPENS.

II.   THE CAPABILITY OF A CONGREGATION TO RECEIVE, WELCOME, AND ASSIMILATE NEW MEMBERS *is the second most important price tag on growth.* It is easier to join most churches than it is to be accepted and to be assimilated into the fellowship of that congregation.

III.   THE SIZE AND VARIETY OF THE GROUP LIFE *must expand as a congregation increases in size. This is a price many congregations are unwilling to pay,* as can be seen most clearly in the single-cell churches which refuse to pay the price of becoming multi-cell congregations in order to grow.

IV.   *High on this list of the price tags of growth is the need to* DEFINE IN PRECISE TERMS WHO THIS CONGREGATION IS SEEKING TO REACH, to identify their specific needs, and to determine how this congregation will respond to those needs.

V.   OFTEN CHURCH MEMBERS ASSUME THAT CHURCH GROWTH MEANS MORE OF THE SAME. They expect that their congregation can double in size without any significant change in the qualitative dimension of congregational life. This is an illusion. AN ACCEPTANCE OF CHANGE IS A PRICE OF GROWTH.

VI.   FREQUENTLY CHURCH GROWTH IS DEPENDENT ON THE QUALITY AND QUANTITY OF THE PROFESSIONAL STAFF LEADERSHIP. A growing congregation usually must expand its staff to accommodate a growing number of members. The neglect of that factor can be seen most clearly in the congregations that have built a very large building to accommodate a much larger number of people and then meet the mortgage payments from the salaries of staff who are not hired. They end up as an   overbuilt, understaffed, a frustrated congregation.

VII.   A frequently overlooked price tag on church growth is the importance of DEFINING EVANGELISM IS TERMS OF PEOPLE VS GEOGRAPHY. *The primary emphasis in the evangelistic outreach of the growing church is on the needs of people,* not on their places of residence.

VIII.   PERHAPS THE MOST SUBTLE ITEM OF THIS LIST IS THE NEED TO AVOID TURNING THE CHRISTIAN FAITH INTO A CULTURAL RELIGION. Cultural religion becomes exclusionary, concerned with its own self-preservation, and is blind to the real implications of the gospel.

IX.   Frequently the need for additional space to accommodate more people is seen as   an immediate price of growth. Constructing new buildings rarely is a means of growth. Architectural evangelism does not work.   BUILDING, REMODELING, OR ADDING MORE SPACE SHOULD BE SEEN AS A RESPONSE TO GROWTH, NOT AS A MEANS OF ACHIEVING GROWTH.

NON-NEGOTIABLE PRINCIPLES

There are some things that the church has that are non-negotiable. Therefore I would like to address these things that should be the foundational principles of any healthy, genuine church. In the myriad of church growth methodologies, programs and strategies, we need to be diligent in maintaining our biblical foundation if we want to be useful to the kingdom. These principles are truly non-negotiable.

As the church of Jesus Christ, we need to be absolutely clear about some biblical principles for growth that are non-negotiable. We may change our methods, but these truths are eternal and unchanging.

1. The Glory of God Is Our Motivation

The apostle Paul told the Corinthian church: "Whether you eat or drink, or whatever you do, do all to the glory of God" (1 Cor. 10:31). We who are church leaders must continually ask ourselves: "What is my motivation in leading my church?"

In our eagerness to grow churches we can look at the growth and its numerical results as our goal. The numbers can take on an importance that is not from God. We are first children of God and then leaders of the church. In both roles, nothing is more important than bringing glory to our Lord.

2. God Is in Total Control

One of the greatest assurances I have as a Christian and church leader is that God is sovereign, which means that He is in absolute control (Eph. 1:11). Many times in my own ministry, I have seen the spontaneity of the Holy Spirit's work, which defies any plan or methodology. Such sovereign displays by God remind me that He is in control and that my church is really His church.

God's sovereign decree does not violate humankind's free will, nor does it make it unnecessary to seek methods of church growth. While Paul proclaimed with fervor the sovereignty of God, he also proclaimed with equal conviction the necessity of human intervention and preaching for church growth (Acts 16:13; Rom. 10:14-15; 1 Cor. 9:16).

When we use methods in obedience to spread the gospel of Jesus Christ, we do not contradict the truth of God's sovereignty. One of the great joys of our faith is that God desires that we might be intermediaries in sharing the good news of His Son.

3. Christ Is the Only Way

The exclusivity of the gospel of Jesus Christ is an unpopular doctrine these days. With around 90 percent of Americans believing in an afterlife, heaven or hell, the overwhelming belief is that there is no single way to get to heaven.

My belief that Christ is the only way of salvation comes from the words of Jesus Himself (John 14:6). The truth of the cross is offensive to the world.

In our enthusiasm to lead churches to growth, we must never compromise this truth. The fact that Christ is the only way and that hell is a real consequence for those who reject Him is not a "user-friendly" concept. But it is truth, and it must be communicated.

4. Christ Builds the Church

The issue of jealousy between leaders of different churches is a real one. I am sure that every person who reads the articles can think of a church which is growing more rapidly than their own. More times than many of us would like to admit, our carnal nature evokes feelings of jealousy and inadequacy when we hear of such churches.

A kingdom mind-set, however, sees things differently. First, all Christian churches are Christ's churches. Second, Jesus is the builder of churches, not ourselves. In His historic discussion with Peter, Jesus said, "I will build *my* church" (Matt. 16:18, my emphasis). We are in the kingdom business, and we all work for the same Master. There is no room for jealousy and competitive spirits.

5. The Bible Is Our Authority

All such church growth resources and tools may be beneficial to you and your church. The tools of church growth are not inherently evil, as some critics imply. But, these tools and resources must always be within the bounds of Scripture and subject to biblical authority. The Bible is our authority, and it is our ultimate church growth book.

A building is only as strong as the foundation it is built upon. I invite you to continue examining these foundational principles.

6. Church Growth Is Spiritual Warfare

Satan will do everything he can to prevent you from leading your church to growth. Every soul saved by Christ is a soul that will not be with Satan in hell. Paul knew that warfare for the evangelistic, church-growing Christian was inevitable:

"For our struggle is not against flesh and blood, but against the rulers, against the authorities, against the powers of this dark world and against the spiritual forces of evil in the heavenly realms" (Eph. 6:12).

Satan and his demons use many weapons to inhibit growth of the church. They can deceive both believers and unbelievers. Unbelievers can be deceived and blinded from receiving the gift of salvation through Jesus Christ:

"The god of this age has blinded the minds of the unbelievers, so that they cannot see the light of the gospel of the glory of Christ, who is the image of God" (2 Cor. 4:4).

A believer can also be distracted from Great Commission obedience and single-minded devotion to Christ (2 Cor. 11:3). The apostle Paul, concerned that the church of the Thessalonians might have lost zeal for spreading the gospel, wrote to warn the people about demonic discouragement:

"For this reason, when I could stand it no longer, I sent to find out about your faith. I was afraid that in some way the tempter might have tempted you and our efforts might have been useless" (1 Thess. 3:5).

In Paul's words about spiritual warfare in Ephesians 6, he instructs us about our weapons to combat the forces of the evil one. He calls these weapons "the full armor of God" (v. 13). The full armor first includes a godly and obedient lifestyle ("righteousness . . . readiness . . . faith," vv. 14-16). Second, it means a knowledge of, commitment to, and obedience to the Word of God ("the sword of the Spirit, which is the Word of God," v. 17). Finally, the full armor leads us to prayer (v. 18). We look at that vital principle next.

7. Prayer Is a Key Church Growth Principle

Prayer should be a priority in the church because God's Word mandates it. Even if we could find no positive correlation between prayer and church growth, the mandate of prayer would require our obedience.

It is fascinating, however, to learn how God is working through prayer to lead churches to unprecedented levels of growth. In one study of churches which had reversed their negative growth rate, the key factor for the reversal was determined to be an increased emphasis on prayer.

The prayers of the early church unleashed the power of God to add thousands to the church. It happened then, and it is happening in many churches today.

8. The Church Is Still Important

One of the unavoidable truths of the New Testament is that the local church is important in God's plan. The writer of Hebrews made clear God's intention for believers to gather and work together:

"Let us not give up meeting together, as some are in the habit of doing, but let us encourage one another — and all the more as you see the Day approaching" (Heb. 10:25).

Even more than single passages, large blocks of Scripture (1 Cor. 12-14) point to the importance of a gathered, united and serving church. The majority of the books of the New Testament are particularly concerned with local church issues.

Despite the imperfections of those who comprise the local church, it is still God's primary vehicle for calling the world to Himself. Indeed the church is the body of Christ (12:27).

9. Evangelism Is Still the Priority

Many times I will lead a conference and begin a discussion on ministries in the church. I may discuss social ministries or discipleship ministries in general, or I may refer to some particular ministry. Typically, I receive a surprised look when I share the most effective means to lead a church in discipleship and social ministries: Have a priority for evangelism.

How can a church with a priority for evangelism be a church with dynamic social and discipleship ministries? First, let us examine the biblical evidence.

Our Lord Jesus Christ, who taught us the perfect plan for discipling and providing for needs, did so within a context that placed the eternal state of a person as more important than the temporal state:

Vision looks inward and becomes a **Duty.**

Vision look outward and becomes **Aspiration**

Vision looks upward and becomes **Faith**

"If your right eye causes you to sin, gouge it out and throw it away. It is better for you to lose one part of your body than for your whole body to be thrown into hell" (Matt. 5:29).

Again, the words of Jesus seem to favor an evangelistic priority:

"Do not be afraid of those who kill the body but cannot

kill the soul. Rather, be afraid of the One who can destroy both soul and body in hell" (10:28).

The historical and contemporary evidence seems to support this thesis: A greater evangelistic emphasis and higher evangelistic priority will enhance all ministries of the church.

A landmark study of evangelists and revivalists in the 19th century found that though the well-known evangelists held to a priority of winning people to Christ, they were also instrumental in initiating massive social reforms.

Yet another major study, in the 1960s, came to that same conclusion. The modern evangelical movement, while holding a priority of evangelism, was also maintaining a strong social conscience. Even as we head into the 21st century, the same evidence is repeated: churches that emphasize evangelism tend to have a greater awareness of social and discipleship needs.

Yet on the other hand, we can look at the records of many denominations that have lost their evangelistic zeal and priority. Their numerical decline has been the subject of countless studies.

Within those same studies, however, there has been a noted decline in resources for other ministries which has impacted negatively those areas deemed to be of highest importance. A low priority for evangelism is detrimental to the entire ministry of the church.

One entire Christian movement collapsed as it rearranged its priorities away from evangelism. The Student Volunteer Movement was founded early in the 20th century upon the slogan: "The evangelization of the world in this generation." Many Christian leaders enthusiastically endorsed the movement as the single most potent force for missions in America in the early part of the century.

Yet, in the 1940s the organization ceased to exist. Its original priority of evangelism had shifted to new emphases such as race relations, international relationships and economic justice. Not only did the collapse of the movement cause a major evangelistic thrust to end, it also thwarted an emphasis on many other worthy ministries and causes.

10. The Laity Must Do the Ministry

The church had grown well for years despite skipping this step. But now the church did not have enough leaders in ministry to care for all the people and to involve new people. Neither assimilation nor discipleship was taking place.

The beauty of the church in Acts was the picture of every believer being involved in ministry. A person not involved in ministry would not have been considered a part of the church. A Christian, by his or her very nature, would be doing ministry.

How that scenario has changed in most American churches!

The most important thing your church leaders can do is to begin now equipping others for ministry. That is your biblical mandate (Eph. 4:11-12). You may have to begin small, working with one or two others.

Then Those Two Will Be Equipped To Equip Others.

Growing up in church and Sunday school, I am confident that I have seen about every kind of program and gimmick pastors and promoters could envision. I have been a faithful attendee of Sunday school during much of that time; a teacher for a few years; a publisher of Sunday school literature and presently what I would consider an unfaithful attendee. With that long-time diverse history I believe I have earned the right to critique Sunday school and offer observations as to how impactful it has been in my life and where I see it headed.

From what I understand and have seen personally Sunday school has been on a steady decline for a number of years in all denominations where it still exists. The reasons for the decline are many – some of which can be overcome and some that probably cannot be overcome. The problems with dying Sunday schools echo the problems of dying churches. Painting with a broad brush, one could sum it up by saying that God's plan for the local church has become so far removed by leaders seeking better ways that it no longer accomplishes to any great degree the purpose for which God ordained it – a place to find truth, foster a deeper relationship between oneself and God, and grow together in community.

Church and Sunday school attendance requires an investment of time and energy on the part of the student, teacher and leadership. When a return on investment doesn't yield a sufficient net gain in a reasonable amount of time wise people move in another direction. In a nutshell, that's what happened to Sunday school and church in general from my vantage point. The good teachers stopped putting a lot of time into their lessons relying more on video and book reviews on trendy subjects to fill the Sunday school hour, leadership didn't develop a sufficient replacements and good teachers burned themselves out, and students opted to sleep in and/or get their lesson from other sources. The same sad changes came into pulpits as well.

It doesn't help any either that the world and technology are moving at warp speed offering options for Bible learning and cultivating relationships that never existed before

Many parents don't like their children going to Sunday school, and would rather they stayed in the main service with them, but the children want to go out, because to them it's a bit less boring than the main service.

I've tried desperately to get the church to re-evaluate Sunday school – it might need re-invigorating, or it may need the rest of church re-invigorating so that the children can stay in with the rest of us. Unfortunately, ANY Sunday school is better than none. I'm not so convinced...

Christians who are studied in the Word no longer have to put up with local pastors of this caliber. One can get simple topical messages or deep expository message from many sources now including the internet and television, not to mention the countless books and learning series available in most Christian bookstores. Because a television show's format demands that they not waste time and get right to the point, I've found there is more solid content in a half hour of good programming than one can get sitting in both Sunday school and a morning sermon.

It's been my experience that preachers and teachers think that people today want topical lessons with three simple points that's easy to recite because they all start with the same letter of the alphabet. I have no idea where that line of thinking came from. They seem to think that expository preaching will kill the crowd, and since it is easier to prepare a topical sermon or lesson than an expository one, it becomes a no-brainer.

I've found the opposite is true, and I personally prefer the content deep so that I will be challenged.

The church was not designed to be a reservoir, ever-receiving and retaining for itself God's spiritual blessings, but rather a conduit, conveying God's blessings on and out to others everywhere.

The holiest moment of the church service is the moment when God's people—strengthened by preaching—go out the door into the world to be the church.

6

What Entry To Your Church Has Been Best?

Sunday school Is...

THE BEST ENTRY TO THE CHURCH

Sunday school classes can and should serve as an entry point into the local church. From the outside, entering the church can be difficult and stressful in determining what is happening. It is in Sunday school classes that an individual can find an entry point, an open door, to the church as a whole. An individual can determine the church's mission, vision and gain a better understanding of what the church is all about; before committing to full membership

Everyone would like to see their Sunday school grow, but what can we do to bring about growth? The following are some of the most important things that Sunday schools need to do to succeed:

Work for spiritual renewal. Everyone's number one commitment must be to Jesus Christ. Does He have first place in your life? In the lives of each Sunday school teacher, leader and member? Before a person can truly be committed to Sunday school, he must first be committed to God, His Word and His will.

Examine your Sunday school's purpose. It's surprising how many Sunday schools "just happen." They don't have any specific goals or plans for reaching their goal. They have no plans as to what they really want to do, who they want to reach and what they will do to reach them. If any Sunday school is to be truly successful, it must develop a plan for the future with both short-term and long-term plans and goals.

Pray for your Sunday school. Urge your individual members to pray more for your Sunday school ministry. You might also consider establishing a system of prayer partners for children, youth and teachers. Perhaps a "prayer calendar" would help remind your members of needs and concerns related to your Sunday school.

Take a close look at what is being taught in your Sunday school.

(a) All lessons should be "Bible-based."

(b) Students should be actively involved in the learning process; learning by doing.

(c) All lessons should include an application for life. Even the best lesson is of little value if the students don't see its relevance and don't know how to apply it within their day-to-day life.

(d) Each lesson should help students face the tough issues of life. If your Sunday school is to really have an impact on the lives of your members, you must help them face the issues of life, both large and small, and help them see that God's Word is relevant for each situation.

Involve more of the families of your church and community in your Sunday school. Families represent a great opportunity for our Sunday schools. With most families containing four or more members, the addition of several new families would represent a significant increase in attendance. But remember, the families of today come in many different forms. As you plan to reach out to the families of your community, don't just target the traditional families; reach out to all families, whatever they may be like.

Put a greater emphasis on the value of Sunday school for children. Every church and every Christian should see the tremendous importance of reaching and teaching the children of their community and seeing that each is won to Jesus Christ at an early age. Examine your programming for children and remind every member of their responsibility in helping to identify and to invite the children of their neighborhood to come to Sunday school.

Examine your Sunday school's youth ministry. Work to make your youth classes and programs more interesting and relevant. Involve the kids in "active/discovery learning." And, work to make the teens feel that they are an active part of the Sunday school by allowing them to serve as devotional leaders, teacher's helpers and in other ways from time to time.

Start new adult Sunday school classes. Many Christian education experts say that without new adult classes, a Sunday school will not grow. New classes encourage new people to come and learn about God, His Word and His will. Persons involved in new Sunday school classes are encouraged to become a part of the total church. Fellowship and friendship opportunities are provided and, very important, new classes can be directed to the needs and interests of its members, many of whom may be uncomfortable as a part of an existing class of "veteran" Christians.

Make sure that all teachers are continually working to improve their teaching skills. To a large degree, teachers are the key to the success or failure of a Sunday school. Teachers must never stop learning. Offer teacher training workshops. Encourage your teachers to read books and magazines related to Christian education and teaching. Hold regular meetings where teachers can get together to talk about methods, problems and concerns. And, very important, don't let teachers ignore their own spiritual health.

Hold fellowship events for individual classes and your entire Sunday school. To a large degree, there just isn't enough time on Sunday morning for real Christian friendships to develop. Therefore, it is important that all classes hold special fellowship building events where people can get together, relax, talk and have fun. Similar events should also be held for the entire church and Sunday school to promote intergenerational fellowship. Such events are also a good place for members to invite friends and other potential new members.

Sunday school is important! It is important because, through it, God's will is being done, His Word is being studied and taught, His love is being shared and His work is being done. Every Christian should see the value of Sunday school. We should want to be a part of it ourselves and to see that each of our friends, neighbors, family members and all other persons become a part of it, too. If our Sunday schools are to be truly successful, we must involve every member as we work to build both our Sunday school ministry and outreach, to the glory of God!

> ೞೕೞ
>
> 1 in every 7 Senior Pastors (15%) considers Sunday school to be their church's highest priority
>
> ೞೕೞ

7

A Healthy Church Knows Where And How To Build Relationships.

Sunday school Is...

Best Place to Build Relationships

As a church leader, I am learning more and more how relationships matter to people. Sunday school gives a person the opportunity to meet and build relationships with others who are at the same place in their lives. This small group time is critical in building relationships that aid in the removal of obstacles and barriers.

Will They Stay or Will They Go? The answer may depend on how visitors experience your church the first 8 minutes after they park their cars.

I cannot remember the source of this information, but it is obvious the truth that it contains should be shared and for those with an interest in reaching the un-churched by helping them learn of their mindset.

Nine-year-old Elizabeth and her mother have been searching with little success for a new church home. They're frustrated, but still determined to find a church they love. Recently, some friends told them about an "awesome" program for children at a local church. Elizabeth and her mom decided to give it a try.

Let's follow their journey.

Minute 1: After parking outside the unfamiliar church building, Elizabeth's mother takes her hand and they glance around for the main entrance. As they walk toward the door, Elizabeth asks her mom if anyone there will know her name. Inside, they navigate a crowd of smiling faces. People greet one another, hurriedly ushering their kids to Sunday school so they can get to the sanctuary in time for opening announcements. No one notices that Elizabeth and her mom are unfamiliar with their surroundings, and no one greets them with anything more than a quick smile or handshake at the entrance.

Minute 3: They finally locate the Children's Information Desk. It's on the opposite side of the building from where they parked, and it's surrounded by other first-time visitors. One volunteer is tensely instructing parents to complete a registration card for each of their children. Elizabeth's mom fumbles through her purse looking for a pen. When the volunteer finally reads Elizabeth's information card, he tells them to go to Room 217.

Minute 7: Elizabeth and her mom squeeze through the hallways searching for Room 217. The halls are congested, and the room numbers are posted on the doors, making them barely visible through the crowd of people.

Minute 8: Elizabeth and her mom find Room 217. An efficient Sunday school teacher stands at the door and asks Elizabeth's name. She checks her in and invites Elizabeth to choose any opening activity in the classroom. Her mom kisses her and leaves. Elizabeth stands alone, overwhelmed in the room full of lively children who all seem to know each other. What activity should she choose? Will someone invite her to join in? What if she chooses an activity center and nobody plays with her? What if no one is nice to her?

Minute 8:30: All Elizabeth wants is her mother!

When Elizabeth's mom asks her how she liked church, Elizabeth quickly says she never wants to go back. They walk in silence back to their car, wondering if they can muster the energy to do this all over again at another church.

We all know first impressions are important. But how important?

According to Tom Clegg of Church Growth Institute (author of 7 *Habits of a Visitor Friendly Church*), "When visitors walk through the door, they'll decide in three to eight minutes whether they'll return." Often, your Sunday school or nursery is where first-time visitors take Clegg's "eight-minute test." The clock is ticking and the pressure is on. You don't have time to waste a second. Read on to discover how to answer first-time visitors' questions so your church makes a great impression.

Where Do I Park? Assist first-time visitors by placing locator signs inside and outside your building. Signs should identify which entry doors are closest to the children's area and nurseries. Use these ideas for signs: • Large letters on the building• Portable metal or foam-core signs staked into the ground• Static signs on entry doors• Plywood cutouts of kids holding balloons marking the way.

Bold, neat signs must clearly identify the children's areas, specific classrooms, the sanctuary, and adult Sunday school area. Put signs high enough that they're readable even in crowds.

Where Do I Go? Put a greeting team in your children's education area. For many first-time visitors, walking into your building for the first time is overwhelming. Train your greeters to shake hands, welcome visitors, answer any questions, and direct visitors to the appropriate area. Greeters create an immediate personal connection.

Will My Child Be Safe? The church is one of the few places where parents leave their kids in the care of total strangers. For many, this experience is an anxious one. Use a central information booth to tell parents what their children will do while in your care. Always keep the information booth staffed with well-trained volunteers. Explain your child protection policy, and provide parents with a secure method for retrieving their kids. Provide brochures about your children's ministry and contact information. If your church is small, set up your information booth with a portable cart and a clipboard. This important touch will inspire confidence in parents.

At check-in, have teachers and volunteers greet visiting children and parents and then share a bit about what kids will be doing in class.

Will Anyone Talk to ME? Provide first-time visitors with a special ribbon or sticker. This signals your congregation that the person wearing the ribbon or sticker is a visitor, and it encourages people to greet them with a friendly welcome.

Will Anyone Assist My Child? Assure parents that their children will be well cared for by assigning an adult "connector" to their children. The connector introduces visiting children to other kids and to the classroom activities and routines. Connectors help kids and their parents feel safe, secure, and valued. They also help kids overcome the anxiety they feel when they enter a room full of children and adults they don't know. For infants and toddlers, the connectors serve as personal contacts for parents so they can find out how their child adjusted to the new surroundings.

What's That Smell? Sights, sounds, and yes, smells are key to making your children's ministry a place to remember—for all the right reasons. Take a walking tour of the rooms you use for your ministry. What do you smell? If there's an odor—dirty diapers, stale food, or mustiness—parents will think twice about leaving their children in your care. Make certain the nursery and children's areas are properly disinfected and tidied. Decorate areas so they're bright, cheerful, and inviting.

What Happened to My Child? Explain your checkout procedure to parents and provide them with written instructions when they check in. If you normally release older kids without a parent pick-up, stay with new kids in the classroom until their parents arrive.

Who's in Charge? Many churches provide a reception area where first-time visitors can meet the pastor or children's ministry director. Create an area where first-time visitors can connect with children's ministry leaders, ask questions, and get additional information.

Will Anyone Even Know We Were Here? Follow-up is important. It shows visitors that you're grateful for their presence and you hope they'll come back. It also gives you an incredible opportunity to get feedback and invite them to return the following week. Consider providing a feedback survey with a self-addressed, stamped envelope for visitors to respond with comments about their visit.

What Does It Feel Like? As a simple exercise, re-sensitize yourself to how it feels to be a first-time visitor by attending a church where no one knows you. Make notes on what the church does and doesn't do well. Test the results against what you see happening at your church and what you hear in the follow-up with your visitors.

The week after Elizabeth and her mom had their frustrating experience, I checked on them. They'd visited another church. When they arrived, they were warmly greeted by a woman who personally took them to Elizabeth's classroom. The classroom teacher introduced Elizabeth to another girl named Elizabeth. The two Elizabeth's participated in the classroom activities the remainder of the day. When I asked Elizabeth to tell me the best part about her experience, she said, "Somebody knew my name!"

She's going back to that church.

Children and their parents want a place to belong and feel accepted. Friendliness isn't enough. The way you respond during your visitors' first eight minutes may determine whether they'll decide to call your church home—or not. What will you do?

The following workshop speaks to this issue and is one of the most requested ones I do.

The Seven Most Important People On Sunday

The only thing that God will ever rescue from this planet is people. Therefore, if we want a ministry of impact and permanence, we better build it into the lives of others. People are our only appreciable asset!

First let's take a look at the marketing world. This information below comes from a leading department store.

Why People Quit shopping at certain stores can be applied to why people quit a church. This can applied to the church.

> 1 % of the customers die
> 3 % move away
> 5 % found better prices
> 9 % convenience
> 14 % personal dislike
> 68 % indifference toward the customers by

employees

The first person that a growing church would consider the most important is the VISITOR

This person is the most important person that attends church on Sunday. His attendance has been motivated by a friend or a deep need. He brings hurts, questions, and apprehensions. He looks for warmth, acceptance, and smiles.

The second important person is the one who meets the visitor at the door. He Is the GREETER

Why is this person so important?
1. First contact of guest
2. One who gives direction
3. To the guest he represents the rest of the church
4. He must be a friendly face
5. He must keep order
6. He gives meaning to the unfamiliar

The third important person is the NURSERY/WORKER

Young parents select a church more on this care than on the doctrinal statements of the church.
1. Must be clean and organized
2. Must give assured to parents
3. Should learn name of baby and parents
4. Writes flattering notes or cards of baby
5. Change diaper at end of service
6. Invite parents to return next Sunday

The fourth is the person THE VISITOR SITS BY

This person is a person that needs to realize that Manners DO Matter
1. Don't hog the pew
2. Don't fight for your spot
3. Smile
4. Introduce yourself as soon as possible
5. Offer assistance
6. Compliment the person
7. Be sensitive to their spiritual needs
   (If they go forward, go pray with them. See they are

followed up on.)

The fifth is the SUNDAY SCHOOL TEACHER

1. Greets student as they enter.
2. Introduces guest to others.
3. Allows for needs to be given.
4. Makes the lesson enjoyable.
5. Presents lesson with study evident.
6. Solicits input from students.
7. Visits all absentees and guests.

The sixth is the SONG LEADER or WORSHIP LEADER

Worship is an occasion to expose the human heart to the heart of God. Music has always been an instrument in introducing us to the Word that is going to come later

The last is the PASTOR

When a special person touches our lives then suddenly we see how beautiful and wonderful life can really be. He shows us that our special hopes and dreams can take us far by helping us look inward and believe in the person God created us to become. He blesses us with his love and joy through everything he gives. When a special person touches your life, he teaches you how to really live.

People respond better to this type person if:
1. Real and transparent
2. Biblical pastors are pastors
3. Confidence and communicate assurance
4. Credibly indicated/aware of needs
5. A person that can handle criticism

6. Encourages
7. Develops a winning team

Remember outreach programs will bring people to church, but the opportunities for growth and services offered keep people there.

Friendliness and the potential for spiritual growth are the key reasons new people seek a new church.

8

Where Is Your Greatest Teaching Program?

THE SUNDAY SChOOL Is...

THE LARGEST EDUCATIONAL PROGRAM IN AMERICA

Christianity in the Face of Postmodernism

Most everyone agrees today that times have changed, and times are changing. The work of the gospel ministry is not easy described, but it's more difficult.   On one hand the commitment levels of Christians has seemingly fallen, not to mention the difficulty of evangelizing the lost.   It's just harder.

John 1:14 (KJV) *And the Word was made flesh, and dwelt among us, (and we beheld his glory, the glory as of the only begotten of the Father,) full of grace and truth.*

Today, my mind is temporarily withdrawn to a trip that my wife and I took to the island of Patmos, where John the author of this passage remained till near the end of his life when he is believed to have returned back to Ephesus according by the Greek Orthodox church who relates to a church that he is supposed to have been buried. In another nearby town Mary the mother of Jesus is buried. This causes me to be somewhat mystified. I find my heart captured and gripped by the power of this book. I find myself amazed at the simplicity of the Gospel of John that lies open in my lap; and on the same token I labor over the profound implications of the Gospel of John. John was written by the "beloved apostle" or the "disciple whom Jesus loved."

More than 80 times the word love appears in this beautiful book of the biography of our Lord as well as 70 times the word witness or some cognate of it appears.

Likewise my thoughts go to a book written by a friend of mine, Dr. Greg Sergent of a Wise, Virginia, who wrote *John the Apologist of Our Lord*. The beloved John was perhaps around 25 when he first heard the call. Now he was well an old man. All of his ministry colleagues faced the hostilities and persecutions of a cruel Roman culture and deaths as martyrs. John writes around 90 AD as the last living witness of the Christ. Amidst rumors and falsehoods concerning the person of Christ, this gospel is historically accurate with a tremendous theological flavor. John want there to be no misunderstanding about the person of Jesus Christ. Church history records that John was perhaps the pastor of the church at Ephesus. A church that was filled with both Jewish converts and Greek converts. A church that was faced in the midst of a pluralistic culture, where the more religious you were the more cultured you were EXCEPT for biblical Christianity that was a church in conflict with Religious Judaism of its day. A church in danger of losing its DISTINCTION in the cultural climate of pluralism. Church members being kicked out of the Synagogue, as well as being involved in a religion that was not recognized by Rome. A Perplexing Situation for John as Pastor.

I find great similarities between the culture that John ministered among, and the culture that we as God's people are called to minister to today. As John was faced with a perplexing situation. We are called to minister among the most perplexing circumstances. ---Social scientist call this culture---Post Modernism

II. The Perplexities of Post Modern Culture
      a. The Post Modern Message
            1. No Absolute Truth
70% of kids believe there is no absolute truth.
72% No Right or Wrong, only what works for you
51% do not believe in the resurrection of Christ.
65% do not believe the devil is real.
            2. All beliefs are equal.
            3. Truth is subjectively defined. "What is true for me, how I perceive and Interpret reality is all that matters
            4. All beliefs are equally true, even if they are contradict.
            5. No overarching meaning of life.
            6. Culture becomes the final authority in defining right and wrong.

      b. The Post Modern Mess
Since 1963 Illegitimate births increased 400%
Divorces have increased 400%
Children living in single parent home 300 %
Child abuse increased 340% since 1976.
This is just the beginning to the great ethical issues we're faced with today.
To the attempts of redefining marriage and family.
   There is no greater question facing culture today than this question, "What is truth?"

Writer's now talk about the "death of truth."   Or as Allister McGrath, pointedly describes culture as having an aversion to truth. With truth laid to rest and buried what is left.

William Bennett describes culture without a Moral Compass.   No overarching direction, vision or goal and no ultimate meaning. Embracing the Postmodern "mood" therefore means there is no real meaning to this life, now or ever. There is no way of looking at life to where meaning can be found....not in our belief system, or way.

John was faced with the perplexing realities of a decadent culture, a Roman culture well on the road to crumbling at its very foundations.

So, Post modern's today, view sermons as merely the opinion of preachers or churches.

III. The Proclamation of Christian Distinctive
A.   Christ is the God-Man as evidenced by his life, teaching,   miracles   Scripture   and   resurrection.   John 1.14 Transcendent---Creator, Sustainer and Sovereign of Universe. Immanent----Christ is up close and personal, man. Christianity answers what world religions cannot answer.
B. Christ exclusively is Savior.
1. Only begotten of the Father....No other means or Way.
2. John 14.6   I am the way, the truth and the life...No other way to the Father.
C. the Christian message is one of Grace and Truth.
1. Grace is God's unmerited favor granted to us.   It is unearned and deserved. Eph 2.8-9 World religions have man either meditating or working somehow to gain God's pleasure.
- Christ in His person was Grace---Incarnation was Grace,

- Calvary was Grace, Resurrection our Justification grace.

It was God's favor bestowed...The Work of *Paraclet* Holy Spirit is a Work of Grace.   Christ sacrificial death as the only means of salvation and we are kept by the power of God through faith in Christ.   That message needs to be a clarion call to the culture.

2. Person of Truth---Scripture deals with precepts and person.

Truth in the Old Testament and Jewish tradition was God's covenant integrity. The Old Testament word appears 126 times to refer to Scripture---that is firm, solid, binding, true. Based upon God's word.   In Hellenism of John it also takes on a sense of "real as eternal".   ---It refers to divine reality or what is authentic.   Jesus not only is truth but brings truth revelation to bear upon culture.

Christianity today with her claims of absolute truth traffic in the truths of Scripture, and the meaning of Scripture and the person of Christ, while the world today echo's the sentiment of Pilate as Jesus stood before him echoing what his culture predominately held. "What is truth?" What's the big deal about truth? Modern culture then has an aversion toward the truth.

IV. A Passion for People

Modern culture may have an aversion toward absolute truth, but modern culture (people appreciates AUTHENTICITY.

A. Make sure that you are in an authentic relationship with Jesus Christ.

a. Genuine

b. Real

c. That is not just Christian clichés and lingo but you are open and honest about a real life changing relationship.

B. Be AWARE of the reality of Christ in real life

Christ at the Well, religious leader Nicodemus, at a Funeral, at a

Wedding, among corrupt religious leaders, with the doubting, discouraged, as a servant. In life...the gospel works out in real everyday life.

C. ASK Christ to give you a passion for those who hurt. Give you his heart to see the world the way that he sees them and to love them the way that he loves. People know if we care, or simply attempting to sell them the church, our way of thinking.

V. Our Prayer

What does a postmodern culture look like?

Most of us here today are children of modernism... Man has placed his hope in science and the ability of human reason, to somehow discover the answer to the deeper questions to man's life and existence.

Herein, the postmodern man figures that the hopes of finding answers in science and human reason are all but lost. So, what does man do, he must look within himself and he looks to culture at large, find meaning in his experiences.

9

A Healthy Church Shares In The Problems Of Others.

Ministry Is...

Where We Share Our Problems in the Troublesome Journey

Every Christian is first accountable to God. After that, each Christian should then have another to be accountable to. Sunday school offers this needed connection. It is in this small group setting that one is able to share cares, concerns, personal challenges, and fears. When a Christian has someone they know will be asking about how their journey is going, there is an increased effort in pursuing Christ-like lifestyle.

Let us begin with their own children because we all are commanded to teach them.

Deuteronomy 4:9:
Only take heed to thyself, and keep thy soul diligently, lest thou forget the things which thine eyes have seen, and lest they depart from thy heart all the days of thy life: but teach them thy sons, and thy sons' sons.

Deuteronomy 6:4-9:
Hear, O Israel: The Lord our God is one Lord:
And thou shalt love the Lord thy God with all thine heart,

and with all thy soul, and with all thy might.

And these words, which I command thee this day, shall be in thine heart:

And thou shalt teach them diligently unto thy children, and shalt talk of them when thou <u>sittest</u> in thine house, and when thou <u>walkest by the way</u>, and when <u>thou liest down</u>, and when <u>thou risest up.</u>

And thou shalt bind them for a sign upon thine hand, and they shall be as frontlets between thine eyes.

And thou shalt write them upon the posts of thy house, and on thy gates.

Deuteronomy 11:18-21:

Therefore shall ye lay up these my words in your heart and in your soul, and bind them for a sign upon your hand, that they may be as frontlets between your eyes.

And ye shall teach them your children, speaking of them when thou sittest in thine house, and when thou walkest by the way, when thou liest down, and when thou risest up.

And thou shalt write them upon the door posts of thine house, and upon thy gates:

That our days may be multiplied, and the days of your children, in the land which the Lord sware unto your fathers to give them, as the days of heaven upon the earth.

Deuteronomy 32:46-47

....Set your hearts unto all the words which I testify among you this day, which ye shall command your children to observe to do, all the words of this law.

For it is not a vain thing for you; because it is your life:

Each of these passages makes the same point, but since we don't have time to study each one, I'd like to go back to chapter 6. If you have Jewish background, or if you've ever attend Sabbath worship in a Jewish synagogue, you know that this passage is central to Jewish life and worship. The Jews call it the Shema, which is the Jewish word for "Hear", as in, "Hear, O Israel." The Jews quote this verse in all their services, and every Jew is to recite it every morning and every evening. It is also the traditional words recited at the time of death or of martyrdom. To the Jews, this one passage, more than any other Old Testament Scripture, sums up their beliefs and their duties.

SHEMA, THE: (shuh MAH) (hear thou) -- the Jewish confession of faith which begins, "Hear, O Israel: The Lord our God, the Lord is one!" (Deut. 6:4) The complete Shema is found in three passages from the Old Testament: (Numbers 15:37-41; Deuteronomy 6:4-9) and (Deuteronomy 11:13-21).

- The <u>first</u> of these passages <u>stresses the unity of God and the importance of loving Him and valuing His commands.</u>
- The <u>second</u> passage <u>promises blessing or punishment according to a person's obedience of God's will.</u>
- <u>The third</u> continual reminder of God's laws. This collection of verses makes up one of the most ancient features of worship among the Jewish people.

According to the Gospel of Mark, Jesus quoted from the *Shema* during a dispute with the scribes *(Mark 12:28-30)*. *"And one of the scribes came, and having heard them reasoning together, and perceiving that he had answered them well, asked him, Which is the first commandment of all? And Jesus answered him, The first of all the commandments is, Hear, O Israel; The Lord our God is one Lord: And thou shalt love the Lord thy God with all thy heart, and with all thy soul, and with all thy mind, and with all thy strength: this is the first commandment."*

According to the Gospel of Mark, Jesus quoted from the Shema during a dispute with the scribes *(Mark 12:28-30). "And one of the scribes came, and having heard them reasoning together, and perceiving that he had answered them well, asked him, Which is the first commandment of all? And Jesus answered him, The first of all the commandments is, Hear, O Israel; The Lord our God is one Lord: And thou shalt love the Lord thy God with all thy heart, and with all thy soul, and with all thy mind, and with all thy strength: this is the first commandment."*

Num. 15:37

37 And the LORD spake unto Moses, saying,

38 Speak unto the children of Israel, and bid them that they make them fringes in the borders of their garments throughout their generations, and that they put upon the fringe of the borders a ribband of blue:

39 And it shall be unto you for a fringe, that ye may look upon it, and remember all the commandments of the LORD, and do them; and that ye seek not after your own heart and your own eyes, after which ye use to go a whoring:

40 That ye may remember, and do all my commandments, and be holy unto your God.

41 I am the LORD your God, which brought you out of the land of Egypt, to be your God: I am the LORD your God.

Robert J. Morgan, in one of his sermons, says three things about Christian parenting. We must carefully perform three duties if we want to instill Jesus Christ into the hearts of our children.

1. Love Your God Deeply

First, we are to love the Lord our God with all our heart and with all our strength.

A. There are two principles here. The first is one of derivation. We derive from God the love, wisdom, and strength that we need in child-rearing. You cannot adequately love your child until you deeply love your God.

The Bible says, *"Dear friends, let us love one another, for love comes from God. Everyone who loves has been born of God and knows God."*

B. There's a second reason for loving God first. Not only derivation, but demonstration.

Children learn best by modeling. If they see in you a genuine, warm love for Christ, they will desire the same.

Do you remember the story of the little boy in Sunday school? The teacher asked him why he loved God, and, after thinking a moment, he said, *"I guess it just runs in our family."* He was following in his dad's footsteps.

2. Treasure Your Bible Dearly

The second step is similar. Not only must we love our Father deeply, we must treasure His Word dearly.

3. Teach The Word Continually.

There are four times when we are to talk with our children about the Bible.

First,	when we are sitting at home.
Secondly,	when you walk along the road
Thirdly,	when you lie down
Fourth,	when you get up.

10

The Healthy Church Sees
It's Greatest Potential For Growth Is Still
The Sunday school.

SUNDAY SCHOOL...
STILL OFFERS THE MOST POTENTIAL FOR GROWING YOUR
CHURCH

Sunday school can once again have a wonderful future. It is flexible. As specific needs in our community are discovered, Sunday school has the potential to respond. Sunday school, cell groups, life groups, or whatever you may call it can go off-site and begin to meet the need quicker than the entire church can. This potential should move us to seek pockets of people who have specific ministry needs.

Sixteen out of 100 persons whose primary point of contact was through a worship service were still active after 5 years.

Eighty-three out of 100 persons whose primary point of contact was through Sunday school or other small groups were actively involved in the life of the church after 5 years.

Assimilation is vital to new church members. If a new

member does not discover new friends, get involved in a small group, and find a place of ministry 80% will drop out within one year.

The following are vital to new church members becoming a fully assimilated member of their new church:

The best place to make new friends at church is within an ongoing small group Bible study.

Obviously issues of faith must be resolved. Hopefully, since the individual is a new church member the issues of a relationship with Christ have been settled. But there are hurts, pains, and other spiritual issues new members will bring with them. We must help them work through them.

The best way for a new church member to feel a part of the church is to find a place of ministry. The adult Sunday school class is vital in this process. Immediately seek ways to involve new church members in the life of the Sunday school class.

Review the following checklist for ideas on assimilating new church members. Some of the ideas will help the church as well as an adult Sunday school class assimilate new church members.

One church said:
We publicly welcome new members and celebrate their decisions.
We make clear our expectations of new members, including our stated mission and values.

The leading changes that affect the American community and the American church are:

- Where people live.
- Who people are.
- What people believe.

We interview new members to discover their needs/expectations of church membership.

We assign/enroll new members in Sunday school immediately upon joining the church. We maximize Sunday morning Bible study for assimilation. We communicate to new members the importance of membership in a Sunday school class.

The adult Sunday school class begins immediately to make contact with new church members.

The adult Sunday school class assigns all newly enrolled members to a care group for ministry and follow-up.

We monitor the participation of new members at intervals of three, six, and/or nine months after they have joined.

We deliver/interpret new member informational packets to all new

Do you know the area about you? You should know the leading changes that affect the American community and the American church. They are: Where people live. Who people are. What people believe.

Do you know the answers to the following questions?

1. Where do the majority of people live in the United States?

2. Do you know the demographics of people and how they reflect the values in our country?

3. What is your church doing to meet the ethnic changes that are rapidly occurring in our society?

4. Do you have a good understanding of the new mindset?

Before 1990 I began to research the changes that were happening in the church and as of this writing, I have found most of what I had forecast to have come true. This with the help of so many other writers and researchers helped me to understand the changes in the value systems of our country and how they have affected the church. That's why am asking you the following question:

Do you know the demographics of people and how they reflect the values in our country?

Take a look at the age categories of people we must reach.

Have you identified the age groups in your area?

Seniors   --[born during or prior to 1926
Builders   --[born between 1927 and 1945]
Boomers   --[1946-1964]
Busters   --[1965-1983]
Bridgers   --[1984-2002]
                 (millennial's are included in this group)

ADULT DEMOGRAPHICS

1.   There are 319 million people in the United States and 254 million of them are adults.

2.   One of the new frontiers for the church is the 20-35 age group, which is the most un-reached group in America. While atheism and secularism are strong in this age group, many are returning to church for answers that education or wealth has not given them.

3.   Of the older church crowd, it is estimated that one out of seven have multiple church homes and that loyalty is much less than it was 40 years ago.

FAMILY CHANGES
1. Half of the American population is single.
2. Divorce is increasing yearly.
3. Half of all adults under 30 will live with a partner before marriage.
4. There are more than 35 million stepparents.
5. Ten percent under the age 18 live with a step or single parent.
6. The fastest growing part of our society is the working poor.
7. The last 10 years saw an increase in both partners working.
8. The greatest social problem in American cities is the birth of children to street people.
9. Busters approach marriage believing they will divorce before they say *I do* -not just once but three times.
10. There is no guilt for having children out of wedlock.
11. Co-habitation is five times greater today outside of marriage and beyond marriage than it was 30 years ago.
12. Parents hand over 20 billion dollars a year to youth under the age of 18.

CHANGING ROLE OF WOMEN
1. The decade of the 80's was the age of promise.
2. The decade of the 90's became the age of prominence.
    a. Major denominations began to ordain women.
    b. There are 27,000 women ministers according to U.S. News and World Report.
    c. Women's salaries have increased to nearly 90% of men.
    d. More were elected to public office.
    e. More are in decision making jobs.
    f. More companies are owned by women.

AGING

1) The over age 65 group has outnumbered teens since December
    i)   1983. They represent 84 million.
2) One half of all people who have lived beyond 65 live now.
3) Over 29.9 percent of the American population is over age 55.
    i)   Twenty percent of those in this age group attend church.
    ii)   The over 65 group is multiplying three times faster than the rest of the population and is the fastest growing age group. IN 2010 it had doubled.
    iii) After 2010, one fourth of all Americans will be over 65 years old. And In the same year, one of four will also have children who are over 65.
4) Ages 55-65 own 68% of all investments in <u>Money Market funds</u>.
    i)   They own 70% of the <u>nation's financial assets</u> and 80% of <u>Savings and Loans</u>.
5) Of the over fifty-five, 80% do leisure travel and 48% buy luxury cars.
6) <u>Life expectancy</u> for men is now 78 and for women it is 84.

YOUTH

1. Today, there are 22 million teens in the U.S.
    i.   The social problems of the last three decades have contributed too many of the ills of this age group.
    ii.   Ten percent of all teens under the age of 18 have grown up with a single parent or a stepparent.

YOUTH Statistics reveal an alarming future for many of our teens. Children of divorced parents are more likely to:

1. Divorce

2. Never be saved
3. Go to jail
4. Not believe in God
5. Not get a high paying job
6. Not finish school
7. Not own a home
8. Not get permanent job until mid-20
9. Not get married
10. Not go to college
11. Not be involved in ministry
12. More likely to commit spousal abuse

YOUTH   50 years ago the top seven problems in public school were:

1. Talking
2. Chewing gum
3. Making noise
4. Running in halls
5. Getting out of line
6. Wearing improper clothes
7. Not putting paper in the wastebasket

YOUTH

Today the top seven problems are:

1. Drug abuse
2. Alcohol abuse
3. Pregnancy
4. Suicide
5. Rape
6. Robbery
7. Assault

YOUTH: Trends within youth culture:

1. Disconnected from adults

2. Increase in violence/bully mentality
3. Influenced by technology
4. Overall reduction of in literacy
5. Spirituality without limits
6. Early maturity, socially, emotionally, physically

YOUTH: Trends within youth culture:
Resulting barriers to ministry:
1. Adults are out of touch
2. Resistant to a world controlled by Boomers
3. Distrust of authority
4. Decisions made without thought for consequences

YOUTH: Trends within youth culture:
a.   Adolescent society demographic:
b.   20% are from good homes
    i.   60% may experience broken homes or have "normal" problems
c.   20% highly at risk sociologically
d.   (5% of the above 20% or 1% of 100% are kids who are juvenile offenders, murderers,
    i.   Rapists, etc.)

YOUTH: Trends within youth culture:
Major risk factors for youth:
1. Family dysfunction
2. Abuse and neglect
3. Drugs and alcohol
4. Living in violent neighborhoods
(-44% stabbed/shot -35% homicide)

COMPARE TODAY WITH 40 YEARS AGO1.
1.   Sixty percent of those visiting your church today come with little or no understanding of the church doctrine.

2. Forty years ago 90% rejoined a church of their denomination.
3. There are 50% less people coming in the car today than the 4.2 in a car 40 years ago.
    i. Today churches lose about 10% of their worshipers each year compared to 5% four decades ago.
4. A church must keep 16% of its first-time guests to grow 5% yearly.
    i.   Growing churches keep 85% of first-time visitors—if they attend two Sundays consecutively.
    ii. Growing churches know friendliness and the potential for growth are the two key factors for the guest's return.
    iii. Newcomers must have at least seven friends within six months of their first attendance.
5. To grow 50 new members you must have 300 guests attend this year.

OUTREACH

The outreach of growing congregations is planned.

They have learned that certain areas of society are reachable and they concentrate on the ten most receptive groups of people to reach:

1. Second-time visitors to their church
2. Close friends and relatives of new converts
3. People going through a divorce
4. Those who feel their need for a recovery program (alcohol, drugs, sexual, etc.)
5. First-time parents
6. The terminally ill and their families
7. Couples with major marriage problems

8. Parents with problem children
9. Recently unemployed or those with major financial problems
10. New residents in the community

ETHNIC CHANGES
These changes will affect the church!
1. The last 10 years have seen great changes in the minorities of our country.
2. Today, our society is composed of more than 500 ethnic groups, and our demographic sources reveal 495 known American Indian tribes.
3. More than 636 languages are spoken in the U.S.
   i. A major difference is our newest citizens come from non-Christian countries with a non-Biblical religion.

ETHNIC CHANGES
The Anglo community:
1. There has been a zero birth change in the Anglo-American community in the last ten years.
2. The last 100 years, 83% of our country came from Europe; however, today 75% of our immigrants come from the Pacific Rim of Asian descent and Latin America.

ETHNIC CHANGES
The Black community:
   i. The black community showed only a 2% birth increase. There are more blacks in America (over 44,000.000) than any other place other than Nigeria.

   ii. It is estimated that the church has only touched about 30% of the black community while 50% of black Africa knows Christ.

ETHNIC CHANGES

a. **The Hispanic community:**
    i.   The Hispanic community has shown an 11% birth increase during this same period and represents about 35% of our present immigration.
    ii. Beginning in the early 21st century, they became larger than the black community, becoming the largest minority group in the United States.
    iii. The movement reaching the most Hispanics in the U.S. is the Mormon Church. Only about 3% of the Spanish community are evangelical.

ETHNIC CHANGES

The Asian American community is growing at a faster pace than any race in our society.

   i. Their birth increase stands at about 18% and they represent nearly 65% of the immigration numbers, which now stands at 700,000 yearly.

   ii. They will pass the Hispanic people in the early 21st century, becoming the largest minority group.

ETHNIC FACTS

1. The Asian American is better educated than any other society in this country.
    i. Forty-four percent of them have BA

degrees as compared to 25% of the rest of our population.

ii. As the Asian community becomes the largest minority group, the Angelo-American community will become an official minority.

2. Two-thirds who emigrate from their country come to the U.S.

THE GREAT COMMISSION

Since the Lord has brought the world to the United States, we need to understand more of who the world is.

If the world's people were <u>condensed to 100</u> it would be like the following:

52 would be female
48 would be male
70 would be non-white
30 would be white
70 would be non-Christian
30 would be Christian
89 would be heterosexual
11 would be homosexual

And,

6   people would possess 59% of the entire world's wealth and all 6 would be from the United States.

80   live in substandard housing
70   would be unable to read
50   would suffer malnutrition
1   would be near death
1   would be near birth
1   would be college educated
1   would own a computer

The following is also something to ponder...

A. If you woke up this morning with more health than illness---you are more blessed than the million who will not survive this week.

B. If you can attend a church meeting without fear of harassment, arrest, torture, or death---you are more blessed than three billion people in the world.

C. If you have food in the refrigerator, clothes on your back, a roof overhead and a place to sleep---you are richer than 75% of this world.in a dish someplace---you are among the top 8% of the world's wealthy.

D. If you have never experienced the danger of battle, the loneliness of imprisonment, the agony of torture, or the pangs of starvation---you are ahead of 500 million people in the world.

RELIGION IN AMERICA

There are 130 million citizens attending 343,000 churches. Please note the following breakdown:

A. 51.3 million are Protestants, attending 300,000 churches
B. 3.9 million are Catholics, attending 23,500 churches
C. 6 million are Jews, attending 5,000 synagogues
D. 2.8 million are Mormons, attending 6,900 wards
E. 1 million are Orthodox, attending 1,600 churches
F. 700,000 are Jehovah Witnesses, attending 6,000 hall
G. 600,000 Muslim
H. 700,000 Buddhist
I. 400,000 Hindu
J. 1.6 million Atheist
K. 2.4 million Agnostic

RELIGION IN AMERICA

1.	It may be that 60% of Americans are religious, but notice that all but the 70 million Protestants (32% of the populace) are a mission field of 60 million. If that 28 % is added to the 40% unchurched, then 68% of Americans are a mission field.

2.	This is assuming that all Protestants are saved, which few will accept. Even George Gallup, the noted pollster, indicates that the evangelical church includes only about 20% of all Americans. He notes that only 68% of these attend church regularly. Therefore, active evangelicals number only about 35 million or 15% of the populace. That would indicate the mission field has now mushroomed to 85% or around 280 million.

RELIGION IN AMERICA

1.	According to the <u>Yearbook of American and Canadian Churches</u> there are nearly 490,000 clergy in the United States.

2.	Of this number, 271,000 pastor our 343,000 churches. That means 62,000 churches are either without a pastor or are part-time. And it is obvious that many of the 271,000 have clergy who supplement their ministry with an additional job. Just how many preach the gospel is left to one's opinion. If every American attended church, there would be an average of nearly 1,000 members. Nationally the average is less than 75.

RELIGION IN AMERICA

1.	To add to our problem, there has been a rise of unfamiliar religions in America during the last ten years.

2.	The New Age movement and non-Bible-based religions have continued.

WHAT WILL THE FUTURE BE LIKE?
1. Internationalization:
- Analysts say that by A.D. 2050, European-Americans will be a minority.
- The church must take cities, immigrant groups, and minorities into consideration as we plan for the future.
- Evangelical Christianity is overwhelmingly white and middle class.
- Our strength is in suburban and rural America.

2. Urbanization: The world is moving to the city. Fifty percent of the world's population live in the cities.

Twenty-six world cities have a population of over ten million, ten of them in the Muslim world.

- Fifty percent of the world's population will live in the cities.
- Seventeen world cities have a population of over ten million, seven of them in the Muslim world.
- Poverty and hunger are now greater than at any time in world history, and some suggest that 900 million people are living in poverty, 100 million of them in utter poverty.

3. Secularization:
- American culture has moved the Christian God out of its consciousness. The media portray a culture devoid of any religious

content or practice.
- On campuses and in the media, the only absolute these days is that there are no absolutes.
- Morality is radically individual, persons autonomously deciding what is right or wrong with little or no reference outside themselves.
- Secular humans long for spiritual reality, as the rise of New Age and other exotic contemporary religions indicates.

4. Technology:
- Our world and our lives are driven by technology.
- Many live most of their days alone with a machine.
- Increasingly people prefer to communicate electronically because it is safer and very controlled. Life is impersonal and often empty.
- We are more connected electronically than we have ever been, while yet more isolated.

5. Individualism:
- Individualistic and self-serving modern Americans are cut off from the community, family, and traditional interpersonal systems that nurtured the heart and soul for all of human history.
- The younger generation no longer trusts the government or any public institution.
- Quite often they have a difficult time with the church because they just don't

trust institutions.
- For the 20-something generation, broken marriages and families are part of the framework of expectations.

6. Materialism/Consumerism:
- Consumerism is the engine that drives our culture.
- While the perils of secularism are more obvious, the dangers of Materialism
- Consumerism may be the most deadly enemies of the church.
- Money talks very loudly.

7. Rootlessness:
- Our unprecedented mobility has destroyed the sense of community that held society together throughout history.
- Churches and pastors need to recognize what time it is and feel the ache of loneliness in their people and their neighbors and know what to do.

8. Moral Breakdown:
In a secular world there are no moral authorities outside ourselves.

9. Conflict/Culture Wars:
- We live in an adversarial world, and all of us take the conflict home and to church.
- Racial, ethnic, gender, generational, family, and political battles dot the cultural map of our time.

10. Decreasing Quality of Life:

- Downsizing, re-engineering, and an obsolescent workforce are creating insecurity that has many younger Americans thinking they will experience downward mobility.
- American people are increasingly pessimistic as our culture seems to disintegrate.

WHAT IS THE NEW MINDSET? – POSTMODERNISM

Postmodernism isn't a distinct set of doctrines or truth claims. It's a ***mood***---a view of the world characterized by a deep distrust of reason, not to mention a disdain for the knowledge Christians believe the Bible provides. It's a ***methodology***---a completely new way of analyzing ideas. For all its diverse ideas and advocates, postmodernism is also a ***movement***---a fresh onslaught on truth that brings a more or less cohesive approach to literature, history, politics, education, law, sociology, linguistics, and virtually every other discipline, including science. And it is ushering in a cultural ***metamorphosis***---transforming every area of everyday life as it spreads through education, movies, television, and other media.

----*The Death of Truth, by Dennis McCallum*,
Bethany House

WHAT WILL THE FUTURE BE LIKE?

The future is an opportunity yet unmet, a path yet untraveled, a life yet unlived. But how the future will be lived, what opportunities will be met, and what paths traveled depends on the priorities and purposes of life today.

- C. Neil Strait

WHAT CAN WE DO?

FIRST
The future does not exist, we must invent it. Creative dreams will have to be translated into powerful ideas.

They take time, education, and labor.

The rural areas cannot be forgotten, but the needs of cities must be addressed.

SECOND
Time is important.

What we do now will affect the direction we take.

THIRD
We need to understand that all of life is interconnected.

A child born in Spain affects the price of groceries in Dallas. A family that moves to Columbus from Denver affects the tax structure of BOTH cities.

A convert to Christ, or a departing from the faith, begins a new set of values which affect all relationships.

FOURTH
Prepare for change.

When we change, we experience new directions in life. Change is both good and bad, depending on who or what is changed.

11

The Health Of A Church Is Found In The Sunday School

SUNDAY SCHOOL...
The Health of Your Sunday school
Reflects the Health of Your Church

A healthy Sunday school is evangelistic

A Minister of Education said their Sunday school evangelistic outreach is alive and well. Class members are taught to mark their Bibles and "go out with the Paul and Timothy model to do one-on-one soul winning."

R. Wayne Jones offered a prophetic voice on the future of Sunday school: "The most important task that keeps the Sunday school as a viable organization in the world today is the task of reaching people for Christ. . . . No matter what else the Sunday school does, no matter how appropriate or good it may be, if churches fail to reach people for Christ, they have failed.

Church growth literature of the past 25 years has offered churches many ways to grow and to reach people for Christ. While these methods captured the attention and excitement of many Christians, Sunday school methodologies continued to be used effectively without much fanfare.

Leaders of churches are keenly aware of the latest developments in church growth tactics. Many regularly attended conferences and read the latest church growth books. They had tried many of the innovative techniques and approaches to outreach, some with great success, others with less success. Yet most of the pastors kept returning to the basics of Sunday school outreach as one of their key evangelistic tools.

Why has the traditional Sunday school maintained its usefulness in these evangelistic churches? A pastor explained, "We simply have found no other way to train all age groups in Scripture; to have small groups in place without creating a new organization; to have outreach accountability; and to have groups which naturally provide ministry to one another within their fellowship."

A healthy Sunday school provides biblical education to all age groups

Lifeway director Tom Rainer said, "The surprising conclusion of a study was that mainline churches were declining because they had failed to provide or emphasize regular biblical training for all age groups".

Thus an entire generation grew up in the church without comprehending biblical truths, the uniqueness of the Christian faith, and the demands of discipleship. Without an anchor to hold them, millions left mainline churches.

Evangelical churches affirm the total truthfulness of Scripture. But mere affirmation of the trustworthiness of Scripture is of little value if these churches fail to train their members in the complete revelation of the Bible. One reason these evangelistic churches continue to place a strong emphasis on evangelism is because they are equipping members in God's Word.

"As we study different books of the Bible," a layperson told us, "we are regularly reminded of the good news of Jesus Christ which must be shared with others." After listening to hundreds of comments about the vital importance of ongoing biblical training, clearly one can see now the significance of the study mentioned earlier. The church that fails to educate all generations in the totality of Scripture is headed for decline and possible death.

Millions will never know Christ unless we run the organization and not let it run us.

A. Healthy Sunday school assimilates church members

No other aspect of Sunday school received more comments than its role in assimilation and discipleship of new members and new Christians. Part of the reason for the overwhelming response came from a simple question asked in the survey: "What specific measures do you take to ensure that the people baptized remain involved in the church?"

Churches said their specific measure for assimilation was the Sunday school.

Over 90 percent of the assimilation and discipleship methodologies of these churches were directly or indirectly related to Sunday school.

An Ohio pastor said, "We have tried closing the back door a dozen different ways, but it seems like we always come back to Sunday school."

The mere existence of a Sunday school organization does not guarantee effective evangelism, effective assimilation, effective ministry, or effective teaching. Indeed, the leaders of these churches expressed concern about the ineffectiveness of many Sunday schools they had observed.

What are the keys to doing Sunday school well? Join us next week as we look deeper into this critical methodology.

I believe healthy Sunday schools make healthy churches. A healthy Sunday school looks and functions like a small congregation. The church has five over-arching purposes: worship, fellowship, discipleship, evangelism, and ministry. A healthy church has a balance of all five. Sunday school classes take on these functions as well. Sunday school classes is to share the gospel through evangelism, prepare the people's heart for worship, serve others through ministry, spend time with each other in fellowship, and take the growth of every believer to heart through discipleship, our churches will be healthier.

Common barriers to growing your church

For almost fifty years I've noticed church growth, and I've noticed there are obstacles to growing a healthy, vibrant church.

Not bringing friends to church

We pray, we ask, we pressure, we motivate, we emphasize, but members still don't bring friends to church. Why? Often, the truth is they're embarrassed. They instinctively know that the services are not designed for unbelievers, for seekers, for the people they know from work. They're thinking, "The weekend service meets my needs, but it does it meet my neighbor's needs?

Fearing growth will ruin the fellowship

Even though your members may not say this, some of them will subtly fight growth because they fear that when the congregation gets bigger, they won't know everybody anymore. So they say, "I like the way it is; I know everybody. If we get bigger, I'm afraid I'll just become a number."

The antidote to this fear is building affinity groups or small groups within your congregation. A Church could say: our church must grow larger and smaller at the same time.

Clinging rigidly to tradition

Traditions are actually rooted in success. Something becomes a tradition because it works in the first place. And because it works, we repeat it over and over again.

Unfortunately, the tradition then begins to drive us. There are some dangers with traditionalism. The first danger is when we make the methods sacred. Another danger is when we forget why we do it.

1. **There are some dangers with traditionalism.**

2. **The first danger is when we make the methods sacred.**

3. **Another danger is when we forget why we do it.**

Your purposes will never change; they are eternal. But your methodology will need to be ever-changing.

I suggest you periodically review – at least once a year – all your programs and then assign them to one of three options:

- Reaffirm it – yes, it's still working.
- Refine it – we need to tweak it so it will become more effective.
- Replace it – You can't use yesterday's tool in today's ministry to meet tomorrow's challenge.

Trying to appeal to everybody

You cannot appeal to everybody. It simply won't work. If a radio station in your community played Bach, followed by the Beatles, followed by a Polka song, do you think it would please everybody or actually please no one? Radio stations niche because they understand people are attracted by different styles.

Now, I'm not talking about presenting a different Gospel; what I'm saying is define your target (the antidote to this barrier) and then do everything you can to hit that target.

Being program-oriented rather than process-oriented

Having a lot of programs can look impressive, but unless you have a specific plan for helping your members grow, they can end up just attending a lot of classes. I believe this is part of why we have people in our churches who have been members for years, yet they show little fruit in their lives.

Emphasizing meetings rather than ministry

In my opinion, you're making a mistake when your number one measurement for health is attendance. If the only thing you ever talk about is how many people you have in attendance, then, frankly, you're a meeting-focused church. Yes, attendance is one of many measurements to use, but it should NEVER be the only one. For one thing, focusing on meetings tends to produce passive spectators who have little time for ministry.

Preaching without application

Preaching without application merely informs rather than transforms.

The antidote is what I call behavioral preaching. This is preaching that focuses on obedience. The Bible tells us to be doers of the Word and not hearers only. In every weekend message, and in every Bible study group, and in every Sunday school session, moving people into doing ministry should be the bottom line – what are we going to do as a result of what we heard.

Not trusting the leaders

If people don't trust your leadership, then you won't accomplish much at all. You have to build credibility, and you have to earn the right to lead.

Authentic leadership is humble, vulnerable, persistent, willing to risk failure – and willing to believe God for great things.

Legalism

Legalism strangles the growth and the health of a lot of churches. Many churches are more interested in keeping rules than they are at winning people to Christ. This will inevitably kill any growth you've gained.

Have Is A climate of acceptance, which meets people where they are and where you want them to be. By meeting them where they are, you can eventually lead them to where they need to be.

Being structured for control rather than for growth

Many churches today are over-programmed and over-structured, and the structure is strangling them to death.

Keep the structure simple, flexible, and ready to meet the all the challenges that the future may hold.

Is there a secret of church health?

Millions will never know Christ unless *we run the organization and not let the organization coast* or *let it run us.*

Your body has nine different systems (circulatory, respiratory, digestive, skeletal, etc.). When these systems are all in balance, it produces health. But when your body gets out of balance, we call that "disease." Likewise when the Body of Christ becomes unbalanced, disease occurs. Health and growth can only occur when everything is brought into balance. "By focusing equally on all five of the New Testament purposes of the church, your church will develop the healthy balance that makes lasting growth possible."

Church growth is multi-dimensional. It is hard to improve what Rick Warren said, "Church health has five facets: Every church needs to grow warmer through fellowship, deeper through discipleship, stronger through worship, broader through ministry, and larger through evangelism."

These five are commanded by Jesus in the Great Commandment and Great Commission, explained by Paul in Ephesians 4, described in Jesus' prayer for the church in John 17, and modeled by the first church in Jerusalem.

In Acts 2:42-47 these five facets of health are mentioned: They fellowshipped, edified each other, worshipped, ministered, and evangelized. As a result, verse 47 says, "And the Lord added to their number daily those who were being saved."

Church health can only occur when the message is biblical and our mission is balanced. Each of the purposes of the church must be in equilibrium with the others for health to occur.

Now this is important: Because we are imperfect beings, balance in a church does not occur naturally: In fact, we must continually correct imbalance! It's human nature to overemphasize the aspect of the church we feel most passionate about.

One church may be strong in fellowship, yet weak in evangelism. Another may be strong in worship, yet weak in discipleship. Still another may be strong in evangelism, yet weak in ministry.

Why is this? It's the natural tendency of leaders to emphasize what they feel strongly about and neglect whatever they feel less passionate about. Around the world you can find churches that have become the extension of their pastor's giftedness. They focus only on what he cares about most. Unless you set up a system and structure to intentionally balance the church, your church will tend to overemphasize the purpose that best expresses the gifts and passion of its pastor. Most churches fall into that they emphasize most.

Unbalanced Churches

The Soul Winning Church If the pastor sees his primary role as an evangelist, then the church becomes a soul-winning church. This church is always reaching out to the lost, to the neglect of the other four purposes. The only goal is to save souls. The terms you're likely to hear most often in this church are witnessing, evangelism, salvation, decisions for Christ, baptisms, visitation, altar calls, and crusades. This church is shaped by the leader's gift of evangelism. Everything else takes on a secondary role.

The Experiencing God Church

If the pastor's passion and gifts lie in the area of worship, he will instinctively lead the church to become what I call an experiencing God church. The focus is on sensing the presence and power of God in worship. Key terms for this church are praise, prayer, worship, music, spiritual gifts, spirit power, and revival. The worship service receives more attention than anything else. You can find both charismatic and non-charismatic varieties of this type of church.

The Family Fellowship Church

A church that focuses primarily on fellowship is what I call the family fellowship church. This church is shaped by the pastoral gift. The pastor is highly relational, loves people, and spends most of his time caring for members. He serves as a chaplain, not a leader or equipper. Key terms for this church are love, belonging, fellowship, caring, relationships, potlucks, small groups, and fun. In the family fellowship church, the gathering is more important that the goals.

Most churches of this type have less than 200 members since that's about all one pastor can personally care for. Probably

80% of American churches fall into this category. A family fellowship church may not get much done - but it's almost indestructible. It can survive poor preaching, limited finances, no growth, scandal, and even church splits. Relationships are the glue that keeps the faithful coming.

The Classroom Church

This church occurs when the pastor sees his primary role as being a teacher. Because he's gifted in teaching and enjoys it immensely, he will emphasize preaching and de-emphasize the other tasks of the church. The church may even have "Bible" in its name. The pastor serves as the expert instructor and the members come to church with notebooks, take notes, and go home. Key words for the classroom church are expository preaching, Bible study, Greek and Hebrew, doctrine, knowledge, truth, and discipleship.

The Social Conscience Church

This is the church that is out to change society. It is full of activists who are "doers of the Word." It comes in both a liberal and conservative version. The liberal version tends to focus on the injustice in our society. The conservative version tends to focus on the moral decline in our society. Both feel the church should be a major player in the political process. There is always some current crusade or cause that the church is involved in. The pastor sees his role as prophet and reformer. Important terms in this church are needs, serve, share, minister, take a stand, and do something,

Generalizations never tell the whole story, and are usually incomplete. Some churches are a blend of two or three of these categories. The point is that unless there is an intentional plan to balance all five purposes, most churches will embrace one purpose to the neglect of others.

There are some interesting things we can observe about these five categories of churches. First, the members of each of these churches will usually consider their church as the most spiritual. That's because people are attracted to join the type of church that corresponds to their own passion and giftedness. We all want to be a part of a church that affirms what we feel is most important.

The truth is all five emphases are important! These are the purposes of the church, but they must be balanced if a church is to be healthy. A lot of congregational conflict is caused when a church calls a pastor whose gifts and passion do not match the purpose that the church has emphasized in the past.

For example, if a family fellowship church thinks they're calling a pastor to be their chaplain, and they get an evangelist or a reformer, sparks will fly!

Intentionally setting up a strategy and a structure to force ourselves to give equal attention to each purpose is what being a purpose-driven church all is about.

Healthy churches are built on purpose.

An Inwardly-Focused Church

Can you imagine a business that never focused on reaching new customers? Imagine Apple saying, "We have no plans to sell phones, tablets and computers to new customers in the future. We're going to focus solely on our existing customers from now on."

For a season Apple would likely continue to thrive because it has plenty of existing customers. But, over time, Apple would slowly lose its customer base until eventually everyone has either started purchasing products from other companies or passed away.

The thought of a business like Apple only focusing on existing customers seems ludicrous and a recipe for disaster, but the crazy thing is that I see churches embracing this "strategy" on a regular basis.

Let me help you discern whether or not you are part of an inwardly-focused church. Here are ten symptoms I've noticed in my interactions with churches across the country.

1.   **Your bulletin is loaded with announcements.** Usually this is an indication that your church is focused on programs rather than people. Programs are competing for people's attention rather than creating a clear path for new people to take next steps.

2.   **There are lots of meetings.** The more inwardly-focused a church gets, the more board and committee meetings there are to talk about buildings and budgets. When people are on mission, there are fewer meetings.

3.   **You don't hear and share stories of life change.** Instead, you're more likely to hear about all the activities that are happening in the church.

4.   **There's only one service on Sunday.** Inwardly-focused churches are more concerned about knowing and seeing everyone. That becomes the higher value over reaching new people.

5.   **If you have more than one service, you have multiple styles of worship.** There's a traditional service, a blended service and a contemporary service. That's an indication that the worship is more about the people who already attend your church.

6.   **The greeters are talking with their friends rather than meeting new people.** If there isn't an intentional strategy for guest services with people and signage, it's a good indication that you aren't expecting new people.

7.   **Change of *any* sort is resisted.** It doesn't matter how big or small the change. Service times. Paint color. Room assignments. Service order. Song selection. Inwardly-focused churches are more interested in preserving the past.

8.   **The church is led by people-pleasing pastors.** The pastors are trying to keep everyone happy rather than prioritizing fulfillment of the church's mission. The first question is probably not, "What does God want me to do?" Instead, decisions are made based on the response of individuals in the church.

9. **The church is attended by pastor-needing people.** The "members" are consumers. They are expecting to be served rather than engaging the ministry to serve others.

10. **People are not inviting their friends.** And your gut may be to teach more on evangelism, but that typically doesn't fix the problem. More likely your services and ministries are not designed to reach people outside the church. When we intentionally create environments where life change happens, people want to attend *and* invite their friends.

The challenge, of course, is that even though your church is inwardly-focused, it could still appear to be thriving. Just because you have lots of people showing up doesn't necessarily mean you have an outwardly-focused church.

It could still appear to be thriving. Just because you have lots of people showing up doesn't necessarily mean you have an outwardly-focused church.

Where does your church stand? One symptom may not be a strong indication of a serious illness. If you identify several symptoms in your ministry, it may be time to call the doctor. The challenge, of course, is that even though your church is inwardly-focused, it could still appear to be thriving. Just because you have lots of people showing up doesn't necessarily mean you have an outwardly-focused church. As you can see, the average range for kid's attendance is between 19 and 23 percent of total attendance. In other words, for every four adults and students that attend weekend services, the typical church has one child between the ages of birth and fifth grade. There are a number of factors that impact engagement with kids. If your percentage is below average, here are some questions you may want to ask to determine what's driving your numbers: Does the number of kids in our congregation reflect the demographics of the community we're trying to reach? Do we have an intentional strategy for children's ministry programming? Does the quality of our children's ministry space reflect a commitment to reaching kids?

Does our overall vision include reaching young families? Do our adult worship services have programming and teaching that reaches young adults? In other words if your children's numbers are low, you can't just blame the children's ministry director. Leadership is only one factor that contributes to the engagement of kids in the church. Does that percentage surprise you? Are you seeing similar numbers in your church? What are some other factors that you see driving the percentage of kids either up or down?

Small groups, life groups, cell groups, Bible studies—whatever you wish to call them—are an important part of many churches. Some churches wrap their entire identity and infrastructure around their small group's ministry. Others depend on small groups for growth. There is a growing trend that even uses an expanded small group model as a church-planting tool. But, what should be the purpose of a small group ministry? The same as the church—to make and develop Disciples of Christ by reflecting Luke 10:27: "'Love the Lord your God with all your heart and with all your soul and with all your strength and with all your mind' and 'Love your neighbor as yourself.'" The two greatest commandments highlight three areas that make a strong foundation to any church, small group, or Christian: spiritual growth, learning, and serving.

To love God with all our heart and soul is to love Him with passion, priority, and trust. We cannot go out into the world and work at our jobs and deal with family and keep our passion for God at the same time without help. Similarly, we cannot be bombarded by media and ads and strange noises in our car and keep God first in our priorities. And we cannot listen to the news and the politicians and worry about bills while naturally keeping our trust in God. We need to see the example of others and receive their encouragement. And we need others who know us who can remind us how God has taken care of our needs in the past.

A small group can provide all of this in a way a large congregation can't.

To love God with all our mind is to learn about Him and to see the world through His point of view. The best preacher in the world is still limited by the fact that sermons have no interaction. With a small group, people can question, give illustrations, even doubt, and know others are listening. Loving God with our mind is taking biblical truths and relating them to our lives. While some preachers do add application to their theological discourses, there's no substitution for having a fellow believer who can look through our particular situation and know which of God's principles directly relate.

The wrong question:

What will make our church grow?

The right question:

What is keeping our church from growing?

-John Maxwell-

To love Him with all our strength and to love our neighbor as ourselves are related. Small groups should be a place where we can freely "love our neighbor," whether through prayer or meeting a physical need. But small groups also provide encouragement and a place of rest so members can love God with all their strength outside the group. Whether the group is formed around a ministry team or the members serve God in individual ways, the small group can be a place to recharge and share how God is working.

God knows we are fragile creatures who need constant reminders of what we are supposed to do. A small group is a key tool to help with this. Regularly meeting with a committed group of believers allows us to reinforce the core of what we believe so we can live it out, learn more about God, and maintain the strength to serve others. Churches shouldn't have small groups to gather more people or follow the next big trend. They should have small groups when and if they are the best way to make and develop Disciples of Christ.

What is the benefit of a Sunday school ministry in a local church? What role does Sunday school play in the context of the church's ministry? Does Sunday school fulfill a vital function in helping the church reach her mission? Does Sunday school still have relevancy in the 21st century? These questions beg to see the context of Sunday school in the contemporary church. I want to give you six reasons why Sunday school is still relevant, vital, and needed.

Sunday school gives the church's DNA a natural, functional, practical expression.

Mission is best accomplished in the context of small groups.

Any mission is best accomplished in a setting of small groups of people. This gives everyone an opportunity for input.

Sunday school equips the saints to do the work of the ministry.

Ephesians 4:11-12 is God's formula for church growth.

"And he gave some, apostles; and some, prophets; and some, evangelists; and some, pastors and teachers; For the perfecting of the saints, for the work of the ministry, for the edifying of the body of Christ."

We have not found a better way to "equip the saints," or do "the work of the ministry," or "edify the body of Christ" than Sunday school.

Sunday school puts people to work doing the ministry, exercising their spiritual gifts, and empowering them with ministry like nothing else. Therefore, Sunday school is in the business of edifying the people of God like nothing else. This ought to cause many to rise up and champion her cause!

1. Sunday school develops leadership for the church.
2. If you were to eliminate Sunday school you would see a

gradual decline in workers being produced in other ministries as well.

3. Sunday school is the foundational ministry from which other ministries are able to spin off.
4. Sunday school gives children a small group experience.
5. Major concerns for cell churches.
6. Many do not provide a small group experience for children.
7. Many do not provide an opportunity for a family worship experience.
8. Sunday school mobilizes the church for evangelism.
9. Evangelism can best take place in Sunday school.
10. It still offers the best place for fellowship. Age-graded Sunday school classes allow Christians to fellowship together through common life experiences.

ഇറജ

Generations are growing up in the church without
comprehending biblical truths, the uniqueness of the Christian
faith, and the demands of discipleship. Without an anchor to hold
them, millions a leaving mainline churches.

ഇറജ

13

The Healthy Church Knows How To Connect To New Members.

SUNDAY SCHOOL IS WHERE...
NEWCOMERS CONNECT, GROW AND STAY

Studies by Dr. David D. Durey is strongly recommended for those interested in assimilation. The following are items gleaned from his writings.

Pick three new Christians who became successfully assimilated into your church during the last year or two. Imagine that you had a long conversation with them, asking how they were drawn to the church and why they stayed. Now repeat the same process in more than a dozen growing churches across your city, speaking also with a pastor at each church to gain additional perspective.

If you had time for this extensive research, what would you learn? Chances are that you'd see certain patterns emerge. You'd become convinced of specific actions you could take to improve the way your congregation attracts the unchurched in your community and assimilates them into the Body of Christ.

Too Many People Don't Come Back

Assimilation is the task of moving people from an awareness of your church to attendance at your church to active membership in your church.

Analyzing into three areas: personal relationships, intentionality, and small groups. First, personal relationships are the most significant reason why unchurched people were attracted to and stayed in the church. Second, churches that are intentional in reaching lost people, welcoming visitors and providing a pathway for spiritual formation. Finally, the practice of providing small groups was found to be the most effective means of helping new people form significant relationships and grow spiritually.

Personal Invitations Carry the Day

When asked, "What attracted you to this church?" over 70 percent of the new Christians interviewed responded by saying it was a personal invitation. Just as Andrew went out, found his brother Simon Peter, and invited him to come and see Jesus (John 1:40-42), so the people I interviewed had received a personal invitation to church from someone they knew and trusted. One of the pastors explained, "Our people are our tool for evangelizing. What God has done in their lives is an example for the people that they are around--in families, in neighborhoods and in the workplace. Our members either extend an invitation to their unchurched friends or these friends visit our services because of what they see the Lord has done in our member's lives."

National surveys have confirmed the importance of the personal invitation. Invitations are the way churches open their doors. Church Growth, Inc. of Monrovia, California, asked more than 42,000 Christians, "What or who was responsible for your coming to Christ and your church?" Over 75 percent said that it was a friend or relative. [Win Arn and Charles Arn, *The Master's Pan of Making Disciples*.

Most people become Christians and enter the church through webs of *relationship*--common kinship, common friendship, and common association. Leading churches use relational ministries to mobilize their members for outreach. Personal invitations clearly dominate the top spot.

Develop a plan to grow.-Then Work the plan!

Growing Churches Create Intentional Pathways for Growth

In the spiritual growth of newcomers and members, using small groups as a primary tool for helping disciples grow. Churches acknowledged adult education as a significant ministry for Christian maturation. One-on-one discipleship was also mentioned. The new Christian interviews verified that all of these ministries helped with spiritual growth, along with preaching and corporate worship. Whatever the format, churches indicated that they had created a specific pathway for spiritual growth, most offering this formation pathway in the form of seminars or classes. Some churches have discovered the wisdom of integrating the formation pathway into the small group ministry by providing both open groups for outreach and accountability groups for depth and maturity.

People Stay Because of Meaningful Relationships

When asked, "Why did you stay?" Over 77 percent of those interviewed responded in the combined categories of friendliness and caring, new relationships, or small group involvement. Fifty-three percent of the responses specifically indicated the importance of the church being friendly and caring. One new Christian said, "I think I've stayed because of the love that they have showed me and that they have cared."

These churches were keenly aware of the importance of personal relationships to newcomers and they affirmed that most people formed their significant friendships through small groups.

Practical Applications

Throughout the research, analysis, reflection, and writing, a number of practical applications continued to surface. Two relate to attraction and outreach while the other two focus on assimilation.

Encourage Personal Invitations.

Churches need to provide opportunities and encouragement for members to extend personal invitations. According to historian Martin Marty, one concept defines the difference between churches that grow and those that do not: are they inviting others to join them?

Church leaders must instill this as a value in their people. Leaders cannot rely on visibility of their church facilities or great preaching as their primary means of attraction. Churches grow when those who attend invite friends, relatives, and acquaintances who are not connected with a church. Wise leaders create events, ministries, and activities about which their members feel excited and to which they want to invite their unchurched friends. Worship services in "inviting" congregations are also high quality and seeker friendly so members know they can be enthusiastic in encouraging friends to attend.

One of the congregations in the study provides a particularly good example of an inviting church. They offer a lot of bridge-in events throughout the year, such as drama presentations, a mother-daughter tea, and a public-garden tour. Also, "every weekend service we present the gospel," states one of the pastors of that congregation. "So, we encourage people to bring their friends. We try to work primarily through networks of relationships so the people we are reaching are people like us. They know that it is a safe place to bring their unchurched friends."

George Barna's User *Friendly Churches,* suggests that in successful churches, members realize that inviting people to church is just part of their responsibility. They are also expected to accompany their guests to the church activity then provide the follow-up.

Over 77 percent of those interviewed responded in the combined categories of friendliness and caring, new relationships, or small group involvement.

Equip Members for Personal Evangelism and Follow-up.

Many of the churches studied equip members and lay leaders alike with tools they can use to share the gospel on a person-to-person basis. There is no substitute for one-on-one discussions, he says. "I've found that a lot of people don't get it until someone sits down with them personally and says, 'here's what the Bible says about how you can know for sure that you are going to heaven, how you can be forgiven, and how to be saved,'" he concludes. Most of the churches uses an "altar call" for inviting people to make a public commitment to Jesus Christ. It then has altar workers available to pray with people who respond to the invitation to accept Christ. Each altar worker who prays with the new converts continues one-on-one follow-up with them for at least three weeks or until they get connected in a cell group. Our goal is within three weeks, new converts will cover three simple booklets with the discipler and begin attending a new member or new convert classes.

Emphasize a Small-Group Formation Path.

Rick Warren states that "believers grow faster when you provide a track to grow on" He also acknowledges that Christians need relationships in order to grow and that believers develop.

Churches could easily combine the intentionality of a spiritual formation path with the relational support and accountability provided by small groups. At one of the churches studied, new Christians are invited to a commitment level called the "Follow Me" stage. It involves working on their growth process in a small group for up to a year and a half. As they continue to grow, they move into the "Be with me" stage where they begin to take on ministry leadership responsibilities. Even at this stage, they continue in an ongoing accountability group which helps them continue to grow.

Update Your Membership Class.

Churches should provide a membership class that will both spell out the expectations of a fully-assimilated member and help build new relationships. The research in this study indicated that these churches had essentially the same expectations of new members as they did for those they considered to be fully assimilated in the church. They help newcomers evaluate if they want to continue to associate with the church, and

Full Assimilation Involves Making New Ministers

What are the characteristics of someone who has been assimilated into the life of a local church? Collectively, these churches affirmed the nine characteristics of an incorporated member offered Win and Charles Arn which parallel Bob Logan's assimilation continuum [Arn and Arn, *Master's Plan. Beyond Church Growth*.

- Identifies with the goals of the church;
- Attends worship services regularly;
- Experiences spiritual growth and progress;
- Becomes a member of the body;
- Has 5-10 new friends in the church;
- Has an appropriate task or role that matches spiritual giftedness;
- Is involved in meaningful fellowship in a small group;
- Regularly tithes to the church; and, Participates in the great commission by spreading the Good News to friends.

14

THE HEALTHY CHURCH IS ...
TRAINING THE LEADERSHIP FOR THE CHURCH

I believe that Sunday school offers an often over-looked benefit: leadership development. Within the Sunday school classes, there are positions of leadership on the micro level. Teachers, apprentice teachers, care group leaders, and outreach directors are just a few. As a person leads out on the small group level, it builds confidence and prepares them for areas of leadership and service to the larger church body.

Years ago I subscribed to a monthly marketing publication from Hillsdale College in Michigan. The following has never left me and has been a simple tool to help me lead.

The Process of Leadership

Leadership begins with the desire to achieve
  _to achieve, the leader must set goals
  _to set goals, he must make decisions to achieve goals, he
    must plan
  _to plan, he must analyze
  _to implement, he must organize
  _to organize, he must delegate
  _to delegate, he must administer

_to administer, he must communicate
_to communicate, he must motivate
_to motivate, he must share
_to share, he must care
_to care, he must believe
_to believe, he must set goals that spire belief and the desire to achieve

Thus, the -"Process of Leadership" begins and ends with goals.

In John 10 we can find three things to do to cultivate relationships:

1. **Know** Them,
2. **Grow** Them,
3. And **Show** Them.

1. Know them

Acknowledge your need for others. *"The eye cannot say to the hand, "I have no need of you'; or again the head to the feet, "I have no need of you"* (1 Cor. 12:20-21)

Believe in the value of others. Carlisle said, *"A great man shows his greatness by the way he treats the little man."* The value you place on people determines whether you are a motivator or a manipulator of men. Motivation is moving together for mutual advantage. Manipulation is moving together for my advantage. With the motivator everybody wins. With the manipulator, only the "leader" wins.

Concentrate on people, not programs. The only thing that God will ever rescue from this planet is His people. If you want a ministry of permanence, you must build into the lives of others.

2. <u>Grow them.</u>

Be a reliable leader. *Relationships grow on consistency.* They shrink on moodiness. Be approachable.

Be a reassuring leader. *Relationships grow in an atmosphere of affirmation.* Most people are insecure; because they need encouragement. Be an encourager.

Be a resourceful leader. *Relationships grow when someone has answers to questions.*

3. <u>Show them.</u>

People do what they see. Model good people skills. People do not care how much you know but they do want to know how much you care. You show them by the way you act and not by what you say. Learn to be a cultivator!

CONFLICT COMMANDMENTS FOR LEADERS

a.   Love people more than opinions
b.   Give others the benefit of the doubt
c.   Learn to be flexible
d.   Provide an escape hatch for the person in conflict
e.   Check your own attitude
f.   Don't overreact to conflicts
g.   Don't become defensive
h.   Welcome the conflict
i.   Take a risk

Leadership may be used in three ways

1). Doing things "to" the people (Exodus 18:14)
2). Doing things "for" the people
3). Doing things "through" the people (Exodus 18:21-22)

Resistance from Others

If you could change one thing about your church. What would it be? Would it be a change in facilities, scheduling, curriculum, organization, personnel, equipment, or training? If you made all these changes at once what would be the results or reactions?

a). Why People Resist Change

1). *Loss of security.* The unknown, the unfamiliar are frightening and unpredictable. The new and different strange and uncomfortable. The familiar is preferred. People like to know what to expect. Change may result in loss of security.

2). *Threatened personal status or position.* An Individual's vested interest may appear to be at stake. Even something as simple as changing from one classroom to another may cause resistance.

3). *Implied criticism of the present.* New ideas suggest dissatisfaction with the way things are done now. It may suggest that the old way is not good enough (which it may not be).

Yet many people are satisfied with the status quo.

4). *Seems unnecessary* or *unhelpful.* For some the present situation is satisfactory. For others it's utterly hopeless. Or an idea may be resisted because something similar was tried before without success.

---

1.   **Leadership Means Discomfort.**
2.   **Leadership Means Dissatisfaction**
3.   **Leadership Means Disruption**

Two words that can kill any new ideas are never and always, as in "We never did it that way before" or "'we always did it this way."

b). Preventing Resistance to Change

In spite of your best efforts, resistance to change will probably exist. How can you handle it? There are three possibilities.

First, you can feel that the opposition is a personal threat and resign from your position with hurt feelings.

Second, you can forcibly impose the change. In spite of resistance and lose your co-workers' confidence and cooperation. If you follow this approach, begin looking for a new staff of workers.

Third, remember all resistance is not bad. It may force you to reevaluate the proposed change. You may change it, strengthen and improve it.

Fourth, express understanding for an opposite viewpoint. Try to see the situation from the other person's vantage point.

Fifth, Admit strength in *others' positions.* Realize that no idea is all good or all bad. If you admit the good points, the opposition may admit yours.

Sixth, Evaluate objections with the individual. Think through each argument point-for-point. It may reveal weaknesses of the objection.

Seventh, when opposition is intense. Shift into neutral. Don't try to win every issue. You may win a point and lose the respect and services of an otherwise good worker. Anything worthwhile is worth waiting for.

c). Presenting New Ideas And Changes

What can you do to help people feel the need for change and accept it more readily?

1). carefully present there exists a sense of dissatisfaction with the status quo. Periodically evaluate programs and structures. Let the facts speak for themselves. Use your records to point out a need for change. Chart attendance for the year. Compare it with the previous year. Let the facts speak.

2). *Let people share in planning for change.* People will more likely accept change if they think the new idea is theirs and they're involved in the planning.

3). *Give forewarning of any proposed change.* Don't spring new ideas and changes on people. Keep them informed as the change takes place.

4). *Begin by making* small *changes.* Sweeping revisions can start with a simple step in the right direction

d). Principles For Presenting A New Idea

1). *Don't oversell* it. Avoid high-pressure tactics.

2). *Watch your timing.* Be aware of extenuating circumstances that might affect the outcome. Take note of' the group atmosphere and attitudes.

3). *Be positive.* Stress the advantages. List the pros and cons and try to answer objections in your presentation.

4). *Give people* a *chance* to *think it over* and talk about it. Give them a chance to get used to the new idea.

5). *Pray* about *each new idea.* Rely on the Holy Spirit to break down barriers.

Dissolve resistance and create a readiness to change.

Years ago I included the following in a workshop I did on Interpersonal Relationships entitled the *ABCs of Human Management.* Perhaps it may help you in leading others.

Human behavior can be motivated

1. Understanding motivation
A). Motivation is psychological, not logical
B). Motivation is fundamentally an unconscious process
C). Motivation is an individual matter
D). Motivating needs differ from Person to person
E). Motivation is inevitably a social process
2. Motivation is person related

A). Behavior depends on both the person and his environment

B). Each individual behaves in ways which make sense to him

C). An individual's perception of a situation influences his behavior in that situation

D). An individual's view of himself influences what he does

E). An individual's behavior is influenced by his needs

F). Everyone is motivated at some level

I). Human desires precedes motivation

j). Motivation is more effective when a man has a clear concept of his goal

K). Motivation is inseparable from one's values, needs, and desires

l). Motivation begins where the person is

M). Information regarding a goals distance is motivation

N). The "terms" of one's motivation are "defined" by the individual

O). One's self image is related to the direction and limits of his motivation

3. How not motivate

A. Never belittle a subordinate (destroys self-worth)

B. Never criticize a subordinate in front of others
    (Destroys rapport)

C. give subordinate your undivided attention
    (Self-respect disappears)

D. Never seem preoccupied with your own interests

E. **(Gives impression of selfishness and manipulation of others for your own purposes)**

F. Never play favorites
    (Destroys morale)

G. Never fail to help your sub-ordinates grow

H. Never be insensitive to small things

I. Never embarrass weak followers

J. Never vacillate in making a Decision

Human behavior is often misunderstood

1. Realities about misunderstanding
    A.). Misunderstanding Is Rarely The Fault Of Any One Person
    B). Misunderstanding Is Seldom Voluntary
    C). Misunderstanding Is Always Preceded By Some Cause
    D). Misunderstanding Usually Affects, Both Parties
    E). Misunderstanding. Regardless Of Severity Need Not Mean The Termination Of What Was Previously A Wholesome Relationship
2. Reasons for misunderstanding
    A). Our Experiences Are Different
    B). Our Perceptions Of Ourselves Are Different
    C). Our Images Of Others Are Different
    D). Our Needs And Wants Are Different E). Our Values Are Different
    E). Our Problems Are Different
    G). Our Secrets Are Different
    H). Our Definitions Are Different
    I). Our Abilities To Communicate Are Different
    J). Our Perceptions Of Expectations From Others Are Different
    K). What We See Is Different

15

The Heathy Church Knows the New Testament Principles of Leadership

SUNDAY SCHOOL Looks At...
The New Testament Principles of Leadership

I like what Dr. Kenneth O. Gangel in his book *With Leadership Comes Great Responsibility* said. A good part of the material that follows was written in this book as well as being a part of my notes since when I was associated with Dr. Gangel when working at Scripture Press Publications.

Perhaps here I should paraphrase John, suggesting that if every leadership principle is available in the Gospels or in Acts were written down, the whole world might not have room for the books that would be written (John 21:25). But several principles stand out with piercing impact for today's church:

• *Leadership is servanthood*. A servant is a person who submits her own will in order to please her master—and others—without any assurance of reward. Someone once asked Lorne Sonny how it is possible to know whether one functions as a servant. Loren Sanny replied, "By the way you react when people treat you like one."

• *Leadership is stewardship*. We need not do a detailed study of *oikonomos* to emphasize the concept of stewardship. In the dynamic parable of the faithful and wise manager, we can see that the manager is placed in charge of other servants not to give them their orders but to give them their food allowance. He holds an absolute responsibility for awareness of the master's will and carries out his tasks within the light of the master's return.

• *Leadership is shared power*. Though current secular leadership literature talks a good bit about empowering others, traditionally worldly leadership centers on grasping, retaining, and using power. Such concepts run counter to the New Testament.

John Stott reminds us that, "Christian leaders serve not their own interests but rather the interests of others" (Phil. 2:4). This simple principle should deliver the leader from excessive individualism, extreme isolation, and self-centered empire building. Leadership teams, therefore, are healthier than solo leadership for several reasons.

The proper climate for leadership development emphasizes a decentralized institutional philosophy. Our goal is to push decision-making and authority as far down the ranks as possible, so that the people who live with actual implementation have a major voice in the decision.

• *Leadership is ministry*. The emphasis on *diakonia* and the thrust of the gift of leadership in Romans 12:8 show us that if New Testament leadership means anything, it means serving other people. With meekness, the church leader involves himself or herself in concert with other believers to engage in ministry. The smog of selfishness and egoism lifts to make mutual ministry a biblical reality.

• *Leadership is modeling behavior*. We've seen it clearly in the relationship between Paul and Timothy (1 Tim. 4:11-16; 2 Tim. 3:10-15). Lawrence Richards and Clyde Hoeldtke sum it up well: "The spiritual leader who is a servant does not demand. He *serves*. In his service the spiritual leader sets an example for the body—an example that has compelling power to motivate heart change."

• *Leadership is membership in the Body.* The leader must identify with all other members of the congregation. In Romans 12:4-5 Paul writes, "Just as each of us has one body with many members, and these members do not all have the same function, so in Christ we who are many form one body, and each member belongs to all the others." Belonging to the others, the Christian leader serves them in meekness.

People Skills Essential to Leadership

In their book *Leadership Through People Skills* (McGraw-Hill), Robert E. Lefton and Victor R. Buzzotta discuss ways to become a more productive leader through the use of people skills. They asset, "A productive leader sees to it that people do their jobs with the skills and commitment needed to produce the best obtainable results at the lowest feasible outlay of money, time, and resources."

According to Lefton and Buzzotta, "People skills is an umbrella term for four related sets of abilities:

1. Sizing-up skills. Productive leadership requires the ability to a) observe what people do in work situations as objectively as you can, and b) figure out why they do it, so that you can make sense out of what you see. This, in turn, helps you interact effectively with other people by selecting the appropriate action from a whole range of actions you might take.

2. Communication skills. Sizing up is only the beginning. Once you've diagnosed your own and other people's behavior, you must devise a communication strategy for finding out what others think and for getting your own ideas across. This ability to exchange ideas is essential to productive problem-solving and decision-making, and both are necessary for productive leadership.

3. Motivational skills. It takes more than communication to get people to work productively. It takes motivation - the creation of an environment in which people do what they're capable of because they have a compelling reason to do so. Before they'll put themselves into their work, people want the answer to the question, "What's in it for me?" It will take your motivational skills to provide the incentive that makes it worthwhile for them to tap into their reserves of ability and energy.

Productive leaders relate to people as unique individuals. They don't deal with everyone in the same way. They vary their communication and motivation techniques to meet the variety of people's needs.

4. Adaptive skills. Productive leaders relate to people as unique individuals. They don't deal with everyone in the same way. They vary their communication and motivation techniques to meet the variety of people's needs. Therefore, the most effective leaders are creative. They shape their actions to fit the individuals for whom they're intended. Lefton and Buzzotta argue that these people skills – combined with the necessary technical skills (engineering, marketing, manufacturing, etc.) and administrative skills (planning, organizing, controlling, etc.) -- are essential to productive leadership.

Understand that most leaders have already learned some fundamental people skills, they write. "We call this using our common sense. If leaders weren't using common sense skills, they wouldn't be able to carry out their assignments. We are not concerned with creating all new skills from scratch, but with building on these existing ones. However, developing better people skills takes both understanding and the willingness to practice them."

You must lead.

Church growth expert Lyle Schaller is adamant that the

key reason most churches do not grow or reach the unchurched is a failure of leadership. And while I do not put the same weight on the importance of the pastor as Schaller does, I nevertheless agree with his basic premise.

Schaller says pastors can be put into one of four categories. The first category includes those "who fail to pay the rent on time or are not able to pay the rent on time or are not able to pay it in full every month." Simply stated, these pastors, due to poor health, family problems, uncertainty of call, or poor work habits, do not carry out basic pastoral duties.

The second category is the "paying-the-rent pastor." The "rent" includes preaching and worship, teaching and pastoral care, organization and administration. Schaller emphasizes that paying the rent is not a fulltime job. These pastors use their discretionary time for activities that do not establish goals or a vision for the church.

Schaller's third group of pastors is called, "goal-driven pastors." These leaders not only pay the rent, they help carry out projects and programs initiated by them or others in the congregation. If the goal is to reach younger families with children at home, the goal-driven pastor may seek to build a new preschool wing, to expand off-street parking, or to develop the latest "hot" program for young families. Goal-driven pastors use their discretionary time to enlist allies and to accomplish tasks necessary to reach their goals. These leaders tend to operate in a constant flurry of activity.

The pastor who does not pay the rent typically leads the church to decline. The pastor who does pay the rent, the task-driven pastor, cannot typically lead a church past 350 in attendance, according to Schaller. The goal-driven pastor, in contrast, can usually lead a church to about 700 in attendance. Schaller contends that we have few unchurched-reaching pastors because most church leaders fit into one of the three previous categories. Only a small number of pastors, says Schaller, are in a fourth group he calls vision driven. They are characterized as follows:

1.　　They see "paying the rent" as important, but they do not believe all the payments must be made by themselves personally. They seek to involve others in tasks.

2.　　Instead of much activity and busywork, these leaders expect others to be involved; "they have high expectations of anyone who commits to being a disciple of Jesus Christ."

3.　　The vision-driven leader believes that the vision will be so compelling that enough key leaders cannot help but be drawn to it. The vision thus engenders alliances rather than the pastor creating them. For the vision-driven leader, a goal is not an end in itself. It is simply a building block to something greater and more exciting.

          a.　Leaders must not quit the fight. Too much is at stake.
          b.　Eternity is in the balance.
          c.　Too much pressure is placed on pastors. Certainly, unreasonable expectations abound. But this battle is part of a larger war.
          d.　It is indeed spiritual warfare.

The vision-driven leader sees few limitations. He truly believes anything is possible through Christ.

Perhaps Schaller's descriptions explain why our data indicates only four out of 100 American churches could be described as effective churches. Very few pastors are actually vision driven.

I understand, however, why many pastors do not seek to be vision driven. They have been so abused, so criticized, so nitpicked by people who call themselves Christians that they no longer feel that the effort is worth the pain. I have been a pastor. I have dealt with some not-so-well intentioned dragons. Sometimes it is just easier to pay the rent than to be verbally crucified.

Nevertheless, leaders must not quit the fight. Too much is at stake. Eternity is in the balance. Yes, too much pressure is placed on pastors. Certainly, unreasonable expectations abound. But this battle is part of a larger war. It is indeed spiritual warfare.

Pastors, be people of prayer. Seek God's face in hours of sermon preparation. Learn to communicate the best you can. Keep a sense of humor. Laugh at yourself at times. Be personally accountable to someone as you share your faith week by week. Seek excellence in all things. And lead your church to something so great that it will be a certain failure unless God is in it. Dream the big dream. Dream God's dream for your church.

16

The Healthy Church Understands Evangelistic
Organization For Overall Growth

THE SUNDAY SCHOOL...
*IS STILL THE BEST EVANGELISTIC ORGANIZATION FOR OVERALL
GROWTH*

Sunday school is evangelistic in nature. Sunday school is the best plan for a Christian to invite a lost friend or family member in order for them to hear about Jesus Christ. Although a gospel message is regularly given from the pulpit, Sunday school gives a needed component. As a lost person sits in a small group, they are able to hear the gospel explained in greater detail and even asks questions about what it means to be a Christian. Sunday school is a safe and non-threatening environment for the lost to begin to explore the claims of Christ. Under the umbrella of Sunday school is Vacation Bible School. VBS serves a major outreach event for children.

THE ROLE OF THE SUNDAY SCHOOL IN EVANGELIZING THE CHURCH

1. Going   = Evangelizing
2. Baptizing   = Assimilating
3. Teaching Obedience   = Discipling

You will know that you have a god-size vision when it meets the following criteria:
- It originates with God.
- It is centered in and supported by His Word.
- It requires supernatural empowering.
- It is grounded in the Great Commission.
- It leads the church to exalt Christ.
- It requires radical obedience.
- It produces natural growth.
- It demands a willingness to change.
- It requires every church member's best effort.

In the *Purpose Driven Church* Rick Warren suggests the following five dimensions for church growth. Since I cannot improve upon them and because they were highly successful for him, I will make no effort for a new set of them. Following are those dimensions.

Five Dimensions of Church Growth:
- Churches grow **warmer** through **fellowship.**
- Churches grow **deeper** through **discipleship.**
- Churches grow **stronger** through **worship.**
- Churches grow **broader** through **ministry.**
- Churches grow **larger** through **evangelism.**

I do not recall the source of the following on the Sunday school but I wanted to share them for your benefit.

The Role of Sunday school
SUNDAY SCHOOL teaches the Bible, the message of God Almighty.
SUNDAY SCHOOL prepares one better to face the problems of life.
SUNDAY SCHOOL teaches obedience and respect for

parents and those in authority.

SUNDAY SCHOOL confronts the student with the demand of God that he accept Jesus Christ.

SUNDAY SCHOOL helps to build strong character.

SUNDAY SCHOOL presents opportunities to share Christian experiences.

SUNDAY SCHOOL shows the student how he can be of service in this sinful world.

SUNDAY SCHOOL brings together those with whom YOU can form true friendships.

SUNDAY SCHOOL gives the opportunity to bring others under the message of the Gospel.

SUNDAY SCHOOL teaches songs of real beauty, comfort, and praise.

SUNDAY SCHOOL gives the opportunity to discuss spiritual problems in small groups

Before anyone can grow a church he must consider the following:

Make a commitment to growth.

Identify and enroll prospects.

Start new classes and departments.

Enlist workers.

Train workers.

Provide space and equipment.

Conduct weekly Worker's meetings.

Conduct weekly visitation.

Teach the Bible to win the lost and develop the saved.

There are many reasons why churches fail and you will find six below.

Why Churches Fail:
1: Loss of evangelistic focus
2: Loss of emphasis and commitment
3: Loss of vision for the total work of the Sunday school
4: Dismantling the component parts
5: Lack of a clear purpose statement
6: Fear of innovation

Analyze your Sunday school with the following information which is a great standard for which you can compare.

A Sick Sunday school
- When your Sunday school ceases to reach new people.
- When your Sunday school attendance begins to sag and level off.
- When you begin to average less than 50% of your enrollment.
- When you begin to drop the non-attendees from your rolls.
- When you receive pressure to combine classes or departments.
- When your teachers become satisfied to teach the same few every Sunday.
- When you see empty classrooms appear, filled with junk instead of people.
- When your Bible teaching becomes mediocre.
- When your leaders lose their excitement for planning, goal-setting promotions.
- When your visitation loses its ZIP.
- When the spirit of conquest and pride begins to wane among your workers.
- When you detect a negative attitude in keeping your Sunday school properly graded.
- When your workers lose their enthusiasm

For a church to grow the following steps need to be considered as it creates the climate for growth.

Creating The Climate

Step One	Drop Defense Mechanism
Step Two	Learn the Church-Growth Principles
Step Three	Dream It; Preach It; Practice It
Step Four	Focus on Soul-winning
Step Five	Practice Body Life
Step Six	Equip Laypersons
Step Seven	Organize Through the Sunday school
Step Eight	Adopt Goals
Step Nine	Be Prepared to Pay the Price
Step Ten	Bathe the Church in Prayer

One of the greatest oversights for a church and which keeps it from growing is the problem of assimilating new members.

Develop A Plan To Assimilate New Members

What does God expect from members of His church?

- What do we expect from our members right now?
- What kind of people already makes up our congregation?
- How will that change in the next five to ten years?
- What do our members value?
- What are the greatest needs of new members?
- What are the greatest needs of long-term members?
- How can we make membership more meaningful?
- How can we insure that members feel loved and cared for?
- What do we owe our members?
- What resources or services could we offer our members?
- How could we add value to what we already offer?

**It takes more than dedication to lead a church to grow;
—It takes skill.**

Churches grow by the power of God through the skilled effort of people.

While we wait for God to work for us, God is waiting to work through us!· God has not called us to be original at everything. He has called us to be effective.

Ten Most Receptive Groups Of People To Reach Are:
1. Second-time visitors to the church
2. Close friends and relatives of new converts
3. People going through a divorce
4. Those who feel their need for a recovery program (alcohol, drugs, sexual, etc.)
5. First-time parents
6. The terminal ill and their families
7. Couples with major marriage problems
8. Parents with problem children
9. Unemployed or those with major financial problems
10. New residents in the community

Why Sunday school Is the Growth Tool of the Future

Sunday school provides a centralized and simplified strategy fulfilling the threefold task of outreach, assimilation, and teaching than staffing three or more different organizations.

    a. Sunday school is familiar Many churches already have some form of Sunday school structure.

    b. Sunday school is a solid foundation for innovation.

    c. Sunday school incorporates the six principle of church growth in one organization.

When God's Word is taught in an uninteresting way,
—people don't just think the pastor is boring,
—they think God is boring!

1. Sunday school is the natural companion to an exciting worship service. Those people who enter first through Sunday school will ultimately become involved in your worship experience.· Sunday school gets people involved in service.

    a. Sunday school provides the small group experience every Christian needs.
    b. Sunday school is not tied to a single personality. Growth through worship is often tied to the personality and skills of the worship leader.
    c. Sunday school has a proven track record.

The People Required Before Growth Will Take Place

A. PASTOR

The pastor does not attract first-time visitors, —but he is a major reason visitors come back. Every pastor must decide whether he wants to—impress people or influence them.

B. SUPERINTENDENT

- Must be a growing person
- Must know the fundamentals of church growth
- Must have a positive life-style
- Must look to the future
- Must set priorities
- Must be willing to take higher risks
- Must have a high pain threshold

C. PUPILS

- Quality refers to the kind of disciples a church produces.
- Quantity refers to the number of disciples a church produces.
- We cannot expect unbelievers to act like believers-until they are believers.
- A church will never grow beyond its capacity to meet needs.
- Changed lives are a church's greatest advertisement.
- We do not have to make the Bible relevant-- it already is!
- But we do have to show its relevance.

Jesus never lowered his standards, but he always started where people were.

"Three-minute rule"
We all agreed that for the first three minutes after the service was over, members would talk only to people they'd never met.

You will attract like you are, not who you want.

Acts 2:
They taught each other,
They fellowshipped together, they worshipped,
They ministered, and they evangelize

**A church's health is measured by its sending capacity,
--not it's seating capacity.**

Dr. Alton Loveless | 211
How Healthy is Your Church?

The Church Exists To:
- Edify,
- Encourage,
- Exalt,
- Equip,
- Evangelize.

The Policy During Growth
- Churches Driven by Tradition
- Churches Driven by Personality
- Churches Driven by Finances
- Churches Driven by Program
- Churches Driven by Buildings
- Churches Driven by Events Churches Driven by Seekers

The Bible gives us the following purposes for the existence of the church.

The Five Purposes Of The Church
Purpose #1:
Love the Lord with all your heart
Purpose #2:
Love your neighbor as yourself
Purpose #3:
Go and make disciples
Purpose #4:
Baptizing them
Purpose #5:
Teaching them to obey

It takes more
than dedication
to lead a church
to grow;

—It takes skill.

To Be Driven By A Reason
1. Assimilate new members on purpose. Grow the church from the outside in, rather than from the inside out.

2.   Program around your purpose.

3.   Educate your people on purpose. You don't get credit for runners left on base.

4.   Start small groups on purpose:

- Seeker groups. Formed exclusively for evangelism.
- Support groups. For the purpose of congregational care, fellowship, and worship.
- Service groups. These groups are formed around a specific ministry such as our orphanage, prison ministry, or divorce recovery ministry.
- Growth groups. Our growth groups are dedicated to nurturing, discipleship training, and in-depth Bible study.

5.   Add staff on purpose.

6.   Structure on purpose

- The Missions Teams— Be in the sending business. The Magnification/Music Team
- The Membership Team
- The Maturity Team
- The Ministry Team

6. Preach on purpose.
7. Budget on purpose.
8. Calendar on purpose.
9. Evaluate on purpose.

Sometime back I read an interesting note on the blog page of Thom S. Rainer. It was entitled: ***Ten Surprises about the Unchurched***

He began with the following words, "Over the past four years, I have been privileged to enter a world that I really did not know very well. It is the world of the unchurched. Now, like many Christians, I have interacted with the unchurched, worked with the unchurched, socialized with the unchurched, and witnessed to the unchurched. But I have been a Christian for more than 30 years. I really did not understand the hearts and the mindsets of the unchurched until recently."

The next few paragraphs are actually information taken from the research that he did when he was head of Billy Graham chair at Southern Seminary in Louisville, Kentucky.

"For the past two years, my research team and I have been involved in extensive and intensive interaction with the unchurched. We have come with our computers and pre-planned questions, but many times we would just sit back and listen for hours.

Our team has covered all 50 states and Canada listening to the unchurched. We have been among a diversity of ethnic groups and socioeconomic groups. We have been in wide-ranging demographic areas, and we have talked to as many females as males. We have listened to the unchurched with modest education, and we listened to the unchurched with doctoral degrees. We have indeed listened for thousands of hours.

The information you are about to read is the very latest in research. A team of 17 men and women gave not only their time, but their hearts to this project. Over the next four issues, you will hear some fascinating information that we gleaned from our time with the unchurched.

But the information you are about to read defies the conventional wisdom about the unchurched. In many ways, it goes against the grain of some "truths" we have been told.

Our research project involved 308 men and women in the United States and Canada. Every person interviewed was deemed to be both unchurched and non-Christian. While we asked some pre-determined objective questions, we also let the unchurched person speak freely. Some of the best interviews we had went off our planned script. And it was in those contexts that we often discovered some surprises. The surprises below are not listed in any particular order.

Surprise #1: Most of the unchurched prefer to attend church on Sunday morning if they attend. Perhaps the unchurched responded this way because that is the time they have always heard church should be. But when we asked the formerly unchurched (new Christians attending church) the same question, they gave us the same response. A very distant preference was a weeknight service other than Friday night.

"If I attended church, it would be the only time I could go regularly," said Al V. of Tulsa. "I work five days a week, and I like to go home to my family at night. And we almost always have some activity that one of our kids is involved in on Saturdays. I just think Sunday is the best time. And Sunday morning is the best time, because we get the kids to bed at a decent hour on Sunday night."

Are there any groups that prefer a day of worship other than Sunday among the unchurched? Though their number is relatively small, single adults and adults who must work on Sunday seem to prefer Saturday evening worship as a fairly strong second choice to Sunday morning.

Most of the unchurched feel guilty about not attending church.

Surprise #2: Most of the unchurched feel guilty about not attending church. Though we did not ask a specific question about their feelings about not attending church, the majority of the unchurched expressed guilt in different ways. These guilty feelings were especially prevalent among adults who had children living at home.   "Every Sunday morning I wake up and feel terrible about not taking Shanna and Tim to church," Mary G. if Sarasota, Fla., told us. "Mike [her husband] feels the same way. It's tough to start a habit of doing something you've never done before."

So, if they feel guilty, why did the unchurched continue to avoid church? As strange as it may seem to a churchgoing Christian, the church intimidates the unchurched person. They Perhaps the evangelistic apathy so evident in many of our churches can be explained by a simple laziness on the part of church members in inviting others to church.

Walk with me through one more calculation. Let us suppose that, instead of 96 percent, only half of the unchurched in America would come to church if invited. That means, out of 160 million unchurched persons, 80 million would be willing to come to church. Can you imagine how many people would be reached for Christ if that happened?

We who are leaders in the church must challenge the church members. When is the last time they invited an unchurched person to church? When is the last time they offered to meet someone and him or her around the church? The answers they give could make the difference in the eternal destiny of a person. Perhaps it is time we sounded the clarion call to invite the church. It may be that simple, and it may be that profound.

Surprise #4: Very few of the unchurched had someone share with them how to become a Christian. And Christians have not been particularly influential in their lives. The surprise is no longer a surprise in light of the previous discussion. If Christians do not invite non-Christians to church, we cannot be surprised if they do not share the gospel with or influence the unchurched.

I wish you readers of *The Rainer Report* had the same opportunity we had to listen to these unchurched persons. If you could have heard how many of the unchurched are waiting on someone to explain the way of salvation, you might have a whole new outlook on reaching these people. You might be surprised that, when some Christians may think "the time is just not right," the unchurched are wondering why we are so reticent.

Surprise #5: Most of the unchurched have a positive view of pastors, ministers and the church. Only a few said the ministers are hypocritical, only after money, always drive nice cars, and have a condescending view of others. The scandal of the televangelists and other Christian leaders is a faded memory for most of the unchurched. And for those who still have vivid recollections of the tainted past, most do not believe that all pastors and ministers are like their fallen brethren.

Perhaps even more surprising was the generally positive attitude the unchurched had toward the church. For the vast majority of the unchurched, the church is still relevant today. Indeed many of them perceive the church to be the most relevant institution in society today.

This surprising response then begs another question. If the unchurched see the church in a positive light, and if they perceive the church to be relevant, why are they still unchurched? The answer seems to be twofold. First, some of the unchurched *have* visited churches, but their experiences have been negative. Unfriendliness, unkempt facilities, poor signage, and general confusion have been some of the descriptions about the church from the unchurched. What is amazing is that most of these men and women still view the church positively after a negative experience. These men and women tend to be a forgiving lot, even if they are hesitant to return to church.

But the second reason for their not attending church takes us back to the third surprise. Most of the unchurched have never been invited to church. And most of them

For the vast majority of the unchurched, the church is still relevant today. Indeed many of them perceive the church to be the most relevant institution in society today.

I would attend if invited. If you read little else in this newsletter, hear the main point. The unchurched must be invited to church.

Surprise #6: Many of the unchurched have a church background. From the most recalcitrant unchurched person to the most receptive, many of the unchurched have some type of church background. Some were members of churches. Others visited for a season. Still others were taken to church as children.

The point is simple. Do not assume that all unchurched persons are clueless about the church. A majority can recall many years of church in their past.

The reasons the unchurched left the church are numerous. Some had negative experiences. Others who went as children dropped out when their parents dropped out. And a number of unchurched tried church but left unimpressed and inspired.

Conventional wisdom about the unchurched suggests that these men and women are total strangers to the church. Such is not the case with the majority of the unchurched.

Surprise #7: Some types of "cold calls" are effective; many are not. A debate persists in the Christian community about the effectiveness of cold-call evangelism. The definition of "cold call" is simply "uninvited." The type of cold-call evangelism most often resisted by the unchurched is an uninvited visit to their homes.

"I really don't mind talking to people from churches," Roger S. of Wisconsin told us. "But please don't show up at my home without an invitation. It reminds me of a telephone solicitation, only worse!"

The formerly unchurched agreed. These new Christians

said that unexpected visitors in the home were rarely welcomed. Sarah F. of a small town in Alabama noted, "I was most positively impacted by Christians who asked for permission to meet me or talk with me. The cold-call visitor to my home was a pain. I ended up accepting Christ through the witness of a church member who took me to lunch on three different occasions. I knew what her agenda was, but at least she invited me to lunch."

But not all cold calls are ineffective, the unchurched told us. We heard numerous stories about Christians who always seemed to be able to share their faith in casual conversations. They were not invited by the unchurched to talk to them, but these churchgoers often seemed to find a way to move a conversation to eternal issues.

"Eric is a trip," Peter W. of San Diego told us. Peter is an unchurched man who works with Eric. "We will be talking about the Chargers or the Padres and, before I know it, he's telling me something about his church or God. I really respect him, you know. He doesn't beat me over the head with his beliefs, but he sure isn't shy to talk to me about it. Most of the church people I know act like they are ashamed of what they believe."

The bottom line of cold-call evangelism seems to be to make the most of every opportunity God gives you. Pray for such opportunities. But showing up at someone's home without an invitation was one of the biggest turnoffs articulated by the unchurched.

"I would be glad for church people to come talk to me in my home," said Millie B. of Odessa, Texas. "I just want to know when they're coming."

Surprise #8: The unchurched would like to develop a real and sincere relationship with a Christian. Our study of the unchurched continued during 2001 and 2002 with a noticeable intermediate point of Sept. 11, 2001. The attack on our nation that day engendered many questions from American citizens, and many of the questions were about God. Though the door was open for Christians to develop relationships with non-believers before Sept. 11, the opportunities increased after that infamous day.

The leader of our research team, Twyla Fagan, stated this issue clearly to me in a memo she wrote about the progress of our research project: "Most of the unchurched that the team is interviewing would respond positively to a 'genuine' Christian who would spend time with them in a gentle, non-judgmental relationship."

Twyla continues, "Most of the unchurched can easily tell the difference between 'drive-by' evangelism and a person who really cares."

I learned how to share my faith by reading *Evangelism Explosion* by D. James Kennedy. The manner in which Dr. Kennedy taught me how to start a conversation with a non-believer, and the way he taught me how to share a biblical plan of salvation are infinitely invaluable to me. *Evangelism Explosion* (*EE*) is one of the more popular training tools in personal witnessing. It belongs to a category of tools sometimes called "canned evangelism." The label "canned evangelism" is unfortunate because it implies an uncaring, notch-belt approach to evangelism.

But *Evangelism Explosion* originated from the heart of a man who is passionate about the lost and deeply concerned for the unchurched. When Christians used a canned evangelism tool to witness to the unchurched with no obvious concern for the person, the unchurched immediately detected this impersonal approach.

"I had some people come to see me from the Baptist church just three blocks from here," Monte G. of Baltimore told us. "I felt like they were meeting a soul quota with me. They just wanted to spill their presentation and move on. But I would've been happy to talk with them for a long time if I thought they really cared."

The "soul quota" use of canned evangelism tools is neither the intent nor the desire of those who created these programs. But many of the unchurched quickly recognized the abuse of these good tools.

If we who call ourselves Christians *really* believe that a person is lost outside of salvation through Christ, we would make the lost and the unchurched one of our highest priorities. And if we *really* had broken hearts for these unchurched persons, we would take whatever time is necessary to get to know them and to share the love of Christ in word and deed. Winning the lost and reaching the unchurched is really no big mystery. There are millions of these men and women waiting for one of us Christians to spend time with them and to show them we really care. Jesus desired that none would perish. In this midst of his packed schedule, He took time to show His love to sinners. Are we willing to do likewise?

Surprise #9: The attitudes of the unchurched are not correlated to where they live, their ethnic or racial background, or their gender. The unchurched are not a monolithic group. That reality came through with the wide variety or responses we received. One cannot therefore expect a certain attitude from an unchurched person from Georgia just because he or she lives in a Bible Belt state. And we could not describe to you the common characteristics of an Asian-American unchurched person. The variety of responses within each ethnic group was significant.

The only pattern where we saw any correlation was related to income. The higher an individual's income level, the more resistant to the gospel he or she is likely to be. Jesus Himself warned us of the power of money to be like a god to us: "Again I say to you, it is easier for a camel to go through the eye of a needle, than for a rich man to enter the kingdom of God" (Matthew 18:24, NASB).

Surprise #10: Many of the unchurched are far more concerned about the spiritual well-being of their children than themselves. A few years ago my research team and I studied the Bridger generation, those born between the years 1977 and 1994. We discovered a large unchurched population among these young people, but we also discovered a generation highly receptive to the gospel. In my consultation ministry with the Rainer Group, I have found that churches that are highly intentional about reaching youth and children tend to be among the most evangelistic churches in America.

And now, in this research project, we found that the unchurched with children at home are deeply concerned about the spiritual welfare of their children, even if they articulate little concern for themselves. Perhaps in our encounters with these unchurched persons, we need to mention their children. Perhaps churches in America need to be more intentional in reaching children and youth. And perhaps we need to heed more closely the words of the Savior, who exhorted us to let the children come to Him.

An article by George Barna paralleled this somewhat. He entitled it: **Knock, Knock, Who's There?**

He started, "Do you know who's in your church? There are many major faith groups in America today—three of which are represented in almost every Protestant congregation in the nation, but to differing degrees.

"The first among the three segments associated with the Christian faith is the evangelicals. These folks base their salvation on Christ alone and believe that all of the Bible's teachings are accurate, that Satan is real, that Jesus was sinless, that God is sovereign, and that their faith is very important in their life. Just 8% of the adult population, they're only one out of every 11 adults who call themselves Christian.

"The second group is non-evangelical Christian adults—those who believe they have eternal salvation through their personal faith in Christ, but who don't believe in various core doctrines taught in the Bible. One-third of America's adults, they constitute four out of every 10 who call themselves Christian.

"The largest group is "notional Christians." These are people who consider themselves to be Christian but don't claim to know their eternal destiny with any certainty and are less likely than others to embrace core Bible doctrines. Notionals are slightly more than half of all adults who call themselves Christian—and nearly half of those who sit in our churches on any given weekend.

"Here's the kicker: Most notional Christians have been attending church all their life! They know the lingo, own the hardware, and even hold down key positions in churches across the nation. But they're clueless about how Jesus' death on the cross affects their lives.

"You don't need to fly to India or China to reach the mission field; millions of spiritually confused people are sitting in our churches. What are you doing to reach the unreached regulars in your congregation?

George Barna is president of Barna Research Group and a well-known speaker and author.

When the unchurch visit your church try to following the suggesting:

When an unknown person visits your church in the future use the following suggestions: **Ten Commandments for the Local Church** by my friend Dr. W. Irvin Hyman, D. Min.

I. **SPEAK TO PEOPLE,** even if you do not know their names. There is nothing as nice as a cheerful word of greeting. One good word brings another.

II. SMILE AT PEOPLE. It takes 72 muscles to frown and only 14 to smile. Your smile is one of your finest assets. Use it!

III. CALL PEOPLE BY NAME. The sweetest music to anyone's ears is the sound of his (her) own name. Call his (her) name often.

IV. BE FRIENDLY AND HELPFUL. If you would have friends, be one. Friends are forever.

V. BE CORDIAL. Speak and act as if everything you do is a genuine pleasure. Try to look happy and you will be happy. Happiness is contagious.

VI. BE GENUINELY INTERESTED IN PEOPLE. If you try, you can like everybody and everybody will like you. Do not limit yourself to a few friends when there are so many likeable people about you.

VII. BE GENEROUS WITH PRAISE, cautious with criticism. Who among us does not need the understanding and tolerance of all our friends?

VIII. BE CONSIDERATE OF THE FEELINGS OF OTHERS. Usually there are three sides to a controversy - yours, the other fellow's and the right one.

IX. BE ALERT TO GIVE SERVICE. What we do for others counts most in life.

X. ADD TO THIS A GOOD SENSE OF HUMOR, a generous dose of patience, a dash of humility, and receive m ministry should be the bottom line – what are we going to do as a result of what we heard.

Since outreach is also a responsibility we as Christian need to fulfill you will find the following ideas helpful in searching for the unchurched.

David C. Cook publications prepared a list of **Fifty Ways to Find New People for Sunday school**.

I am sure they would like for you to know them.

FIFTY WAYS TO FIND NEW PEOPLE FOR SUNDAY SCHOOL

1. List unchurched families from Vacation Bible School records.
2. Conduct an inside census.
3. Locate newcomers by calling all new listings in phone directory.
4. Update a former community survey.
6. Compare church recreation participants to Sunday school rolls.
7. Subscribe to newcomer service for information.
8. Locate homebound by publishing lists and asking for update.
9. Use telephone directory to survey an entire telephone exchange.
10. Subscribe to Legal News for information on new homeowners.
11. Canvas university dormitories for unchurched.
12. Check college admissions office for church preferences of students.
13. Request information from managers of mobile home parks.
14. Call college placement offices for newly employed.
15. Identify shift workers through church survey.
16. Gather information on those who work in hospitals.
17. Survey membership for those who are food service workers.
18. Survey membership for those who are hotel and motel employees.
19. List church members who work on Sundays.
20. Contact international clubs for information on foreign students.
21. Confer with military base chaplains for unchurched families.
22. Use the door-to-door survey to locate unchurched people.
23. Request business people to identify associates who are

unchurched.

24. Request church members to identify neighbors who are unchurched.
25. Identify unenrolled parents of children enrolled in Sunday school.
26. Identify unchurched parents of children enrolled in church day schools, kindergartens, and day-care centers.
27. Request mail response from radio audience.
28. Secure names from Dial-a-Devotional service.
29. Survey by phone newcomers listed by utilities turn-ons.
30. Use "I Know a Prospect" cards throughout the church.
31. Follow up on information received from Sunday school visitors.
32. Follow up on information received from church worship visitors.
33. Request information on newcomers from real estate agents.
34. Secure information on the families of mentally retarded.
35. Check church roll against Sunday school roll for Bible study prospects.
36. Identify unchurched persons in one's vocation, discipline, and/or Professional club.
37. Locate persons in correctional institutions desiring Bible study.
38. Glean local hospital reports in newspapers for names of new babies.
39. Check the hospital reports in newspapers for names of new babies.
40. Enclose a "return card" in graduates' congratulations.
41. Send congratulations to those who have been reported achieving any public recognition.
42. Check all family members of babies enrolled in Cradle Roll department.
43. Use cross-reference directories to survey apartment houses.
44. Provide Outreach-Ministry forms for ongoing prospect reporting.
45. Provide guest book in church lobby to identify visitors to weddings, funerals, and other meetings at the church.
46. Register attendance of every person who attends revival.
47. Provide social events for parents without partners.

48. Secure information from administrators of senior adult centers.
49. Conduct an age-group hunt of a specific area and age.
50. Use special registration forms for church events such as concerts, drama etc.

Not only do I believe you need the help of knowing who good prospects are and how to find them but you should also know there equations you should learn for outreach. Note the ratios for each.

CHURCH GROWTH RATIOS

Friendship Ratio - 1:7

-- Each new convert should be able to identify at least seven friends in the church within the first six months. Sunday school proponents have long emphasized the necessity of friendships in the small-group context of Sunday school as it relates to shutting the back door of the church.

There should be at least 60 roles and tasks available for every 100 members in the church.

Role/Task Ratio - 60:100

-- There should be at least 60 roles and tasks available for every 100 members in the church. While I have never encountered any ratios mentioned, I have been impressed with the recognition that the closely age-graded Sunday school provides numerous opportunities to work. J. N. Barnette wrote: "It is possible to provide in the Sunday school a place of attractive, worthwhile service for the majority of the church members."

Group Ratio - 7:100

-- There should be at least 7 groups in a church for every 100 members. If you will divide the 100 by 7 you will find that the size of the group should be around 14. Does that number ring any bells? The adult Sunday school class should have about 25 enrolled members which will allow for an average attendance of about 13.

New Group Ratio - 1:5

-- Of the groups that now exist in a church, one of every five should have been started in the past two years. This ratio emphasizes once again the principle that new groups grow more quickly. We looked at this earlier. I would interject one other interesting reflection at this point. The Sunday school emphasis on yearly promotion would enable every church to meet and exceed this new group ratio.

Board Ratio - 1:5

-- One of every five board members should have joined the church within the last two years. New board and committee members bring vitality. A. V. Washburn's chapter "A Church Enlisting and Developing Sunday school Workers" lays great emphasis on seeking out and training and involving new workers. In that same chapter he gave an interesting ratio of his own. Washburn suggested that we can reach ten people for every one leader. If the church desires to grow, the ratio should be one to six.

Staff Ratio - 1:150

-- A church should have one full-time staff member for every 150 persons in worship. While this is not particularly addressed by Sunday school writers, I have added it for sake of completeness.

Visitor Ratio - 3:10

-- Of the first-time visitors who live in the church's ministry area, three of every ten should be actively involved within a year. Sunday school writers deal frequently with the follow-up of visitors through the Sunday school.

"Great Commission" Ratio

- 3:5 -- At least three of every five elected officers should have a "Great Commission" conscience. Anyone reading Early Sunday school authors will quickly recognize that the Great Commission was seen as the marching order of the church. They expected all those who led in the Sunday school to be "Great Commission" thinkers.

17

Know The Best Place To Teach Doctrine

THE SUNDAY SCHOOL OFFERS...
The Best Place to Teach Doctrine

I believe Sunday school because real ministry happens there; both inward and outward. As a result of Sunday school classes being smaller, a more aware and focused care for the members can take place. Inwardly, classes minister to each other in times of sorrow, joy, and need. Outwardly, Sunday school classes themselves have the ability to minister to those outside in the community through mission projects. When this happens at the micro level, the excitement and passion spreads to the macro level.

In my files I ran across a research done by the Rainer organization called, **The importance of doctrine to church growth** that was done in 2004. I think it bare sharing. The following is the complete article.

Their organization interviewed with more than 300 formerly unchurched people indicated that among the issues important to them, even when they were lost and unchurched, is the issue of doctrine.

"Even before I became a Christian," Cheryl S. told us, "I was really interested in what churches believed. I had enough common sense to know that they weren't all exactly alike. I wanted to find a church that would stick to their guns on their beliefs."

Surprisingly, the formerly unchurched indicated a greater interest in doctrine than longer-term Christians. Some 91 percent of the formerly unchurched thought that doctrine was important; 89 percent of those who transferred from another church expressed the same sentiments.

The formerly unchurched, however, were not just interested in the facts of the doctrine; they were insistent that the churches should be uncompromising in their stand. These facts fly in the face of an increasingly pluralistic and theologically tolerant culture.

It seems as if when one takes the step from being firmly unchurched to at least being an inquirer, attitudes change. The seeker desires to discover truth and a conviction among Christians about the reality of God, Jesus, and the entire supernatural realm.

Jorge C. spoke rather bluntly about the issue: "I visited a few churches before I became a Christian. Man, some of them made me want to vomit! They didn't show any more conviction about their beliefs than I did. And I was lost and going to hell!"

The formerly unchurched were clear. They not only were interested in learning about doctrine, they were attracted to conservative, evangelical churches that were uncompromising in their beliefs.

Dean Kelley was right. Churches that are lukewarm in their doctrinal conviction do not attract the unchurched.

In 1972 Dean Kelley wrote a landmark and hotly debated

book called "Why Conservative Churches Are Growing." The very fact that Kelley, an executive with the liberal National Council of Churches, even acknowledged the growth of conservative churches was significant. But Kelley went further, describing the characteristics of these conservative churches. The first characteristic, obviously the most important to Kelley, was "a total belief system." In simple terms, Kelley was saying that conservative churches believe the Bible and make no apology for it.

Kelly further described four other distinguishing features of conservative churches:

The formerly unchurched we interviewed probably never read "Why Conservative Churches Are Growing." But they echoed in sentiment what Kelley articulated in facts: **Churches that are lukewarm in their doctrinal conviction do not attract the unchurched.**

"I can find plenty of compromise in the world," Rob M. of West Virginia told us, "but I expect the church to stand for something."

Looking for absolutes

Because almost nine out of 10 formerly unchurched told us that doctrine was the major factor in their choosing a church, we delved further into this issue. "Why," we asked, "is doctrine so important to you?" The most frequent response was a desire to know truth or absolutes.

Janet D. is a stay-at-home mom living in the Cincinnati area. She was raised in a home with no church background, and said her parents are "friendly agnostics." Janet's parents never communicated any particular sense of truth to her.

"I'm just not sure on what authority they base their values," she said.

Janet and Lyle were married seven years ago, and they now have two sons. Janet expressed to Lyle her desire to find for their children some type of environment that had a clearly defined value system. Lyle had grown up occasionally attending a Southern Baptist church across the Ohio River in Kentucky. An affable fellow, according to Janet, Lyle was glad to help her on this quest.

"I began my search for truth under the guise that my kids needed clear boundaries," Janet said. "But the search was really for me." Neither Janet nor Lyle were Christians at this point.

Janet described the frustration of her upbringing: "My parents didn't have a clue. The schools I attended, from kindergarten to college, almost seemed to have a disdain for absolutes. And all the friends I hung around with were as clueless as I was. Here I was 29 years old, and I felt like a kid lost in a big store."

Naturally religion and churches were on Janet's mind as paths to pursue. But she did not know where to turn. She was fortunate. The first church she and Lyle visited gave her the answers she had been seeking. "God must have been looking after me. I could have gone a thousand different ways. But I just remembered seeing this church from the Interstate and thinking that it looked nice," she reflected.

The church of choice was a warm, evangelical, nondenominational community church. Attendance was about 600, and the church put a lot of resources into its children's ministry. Both Matt and Brett, Janet and Lyle's sons, instantly connected with the church. And Janet knew she had found the perfect place right away.

"It was unbelievable. The church made clear their positions on doctrinal issues in their publications. Pastor Eric spoke clearly about the church's position in his sermon. I had to decide that either all of the people at the church were deluded or that I had found the answers I was seeking. I chose the latter."

Janet and Lyle accepted Christ a few weeks later. Doctrine had brought them to the church, and it keeps them there today. Frankly, most of the stories we heard from the formerly unchurched are not like Janet's story. Most of those we interviewed did not understand explicitly that they were searching for absolutes as they visited churches.

Selena T., for example, was one of those rare cases in which her husband became a Christian before she did -- six months earlier to be exact. She started attending the worship services to be with her husband, and she was immediately impacted by the pastor's sermons.

"Jeff is an incredible preacher," Selena said. "His style of preaching and delivery is good, but the content of his sermons is great. I began listening carefully to his words and realized that I had never really considered what I believed about God or eternal matters.

"More than anything else, I became a Christian because I was drawn to a church that taught clearly the Word of God. That's why I answered in the first interview that I identified with the beliefs of the church."

Plainly, a clear and constant stance on doctrine was important to the formerly unchurched in their decision to attend and to eventually join a church. But as we will see, it is not the doctrine alone that attracted the formerly unchurched.

Now back to Rainer:

"In nearly half of our interviews with the formerly unchurched, we heard some indication that certitude was an important reason they chose a church.

One question we routinely asked in our interviews was, "What brought you back to the church?" We received answers such as the following relating to the issue of certitude:

In some of my church consultations, interviewing the pastor briefly or listening to a sermon tells me immediately what one problem may be — no sense of certitude. The words may be similar to another pastor's sermons, but conviction is lacking. The formerly unchurched told us with clarity that they recognized certitude or lack of certitude even before they became Christians.

Sean R. is a civil engineer in a mid-sized town in South Carolina. Sean was one of many formerly unchurched men who told us that their wives were the single greatest influence in getting them to visit churches.

"Marilyn was lovingly persistent, I always say," Sean said. "She didn't nag me, but I had no doubt that she wanted me to visit church with her. Every now and then, I would be the good husband and follow her to a church."

Sean continued, "I tell you, Thom, I honestly can't remember anything about the other churches I visited. Maybe I was so spiritually dead that I don't remember anything about them. Or maybe the churches were so dead that they made no impact on me."

Everything changed when Sean and Marilyn visited a church where the preacher spoke with certitude. "I was mesmerized by the sermon," Sean said. "And it wasn't just [the] delivery. The first time I heard [the preacher] I thought, 'this guy really believes this stuff.' I guess I really surprised Marilyn when I told her I wanted to go back for another visit."

Sean returned to church several times. The conviction with which the minister spoke convinced Sean to explore Christianity. Six months after their first visit, Sean accepted Christ. When we spoke to him, his enthusiasm for his faith was obvious.

"I get excited thinking about where I am now. But I also know that there are a lot of churches out there where no conviction exists. I've been to some of them. You're never going to convince a lost person to become a Christian unless the church is totally sold out on its beliefs. Man! There sure are a lot of wishy-washy churches out there."

Anecdotally, the formerly unchurched seemed to be more cognizant of the certitude of belief present in churches than did the transfer churched. Stories like Sean's were not uncommon.

And in many cases, the formerly unchurched told us that the evidence of clarity and conviction of doctrine was most obvious in the pastor. Studies done by Southern Baptists did the following: **The Pastor, doctrine, and certitude.**

We heard hundreds of comments about doctrine from the 353 formerly unchurched we interviewed. Some reflected on written documents in which the church made clear its doctrinal position. Others told of how a small group or Sunday school class communicated clearly a conviction or stand on doctrinal positions. A few spoke of conversations they had with church members in which doctrinal conviction was evident. Yet the overwhelming number of comments regarding doctrinal certitude was tied to the pastor.

First, these new Christians told us, the pastors mentioned doctrinal issues with frequency.

"One thing that impressed me about Mark [the pastor] the first time I came to Southwick Church was his willingness to tackle tough issues in his sermon," Bill P. of Maryland told us. "I remember the first sermon really well. It was about Christ being the only way of salvation. He hit that issue straight on. And honestly, that was something I had been struggling with."

Bill told us he heard the pastor take on many doctrinal issues over the course of his visits the next several weeks. "It seemed like every opportunity Mark had, he mentioned something about biblical beliefs," Bill said.

We heard many similar stories from the formerly unchurched. Pastors considered the understanding of major doctrines critical to the health of the church. Thus, the formerly unchurched heard doctrinal issues with frequency. Bill continued, "One of the things that attracted me to Southwick was that you had no doubt where the church stood. Just listen to Mark a few weeks and you'll know."

Secondly, the formerly unchurched most readily noticed

the level of conviction when the pastor spoke.

Bill, like many of our interviewees, did not hesitate to speak his mind. In the course of our interview about Southwick, the church he joined, Bill decided to tell us about a church he did not join.

"I didn't have a church background," Bill said, "but I sure could tell a lot about churches after a visit or two. There was this one church where the preacher went through all sorts of gyrations to say nothing. It was like he was afraid he would offend somebody. Personally, I was offended that he was such a dud. I could've turned on the TV and watched "The Simpsons"and learned as much about the Bible!"

Bill became more animated in his conversation. "Why do these guys even get into the ministry if they don't believe anything? It seems like it would be a matter of integrity for them to believe in what they do. What a shame!"

We can say with a high degree of certainty that clearly articulated doctrine attracts the unchurched. And we can also say, based on the results thus far, that doctrinal conviction assimilates the formerly unchurched as well. How then does doctrine affect the closing of the back door?

First, we were told, no one desires to be a part of an organization or cause based on uncertainty or ambiguity.

"Why should I waste my time being a part of something that doesn't really make a difference?" said Leslie C. of Missouri. To the contrary, doctrinal certainty and clarity engender commitment. A cause or a purpose is evident, and many desire to be a part of the cause.

One of the reasons the formerly unchurched were attracted to the church they joined was the church's unambiguous declaration of absolutes

Second, one of the reasons the formerly unchurched were attracted to the church they joined was the church's unambiguous declaration of absolutes. In a world of relativity, many seekers desire to know that a black-and-white reality does exist. That same clarity of absolutes that attracted the unchurched keeps them in the church.   Third, churches with doctrinal certitude tend to be activists in their beliefs. When these churches know with certainty that salvation comes only through Christ and believe that those without a personal relationship with him are hell-bound, they are more likely to be evangelistic. Their evangelistic passion reflects their conviction about what they believe. And their continuing role of activism tends to keep those who desire to be a part of a greater cause.

Speaking the truth in love

In all of our 353 interviews with the formerly unchurched, we never heard the effective churches described as harsh, legalistic or the like. These churches were firm in their convictions, said the formerly unchurched, but were also gentle in spirit. As indicated last week, this characteristic was evident in the pastors of the churches, but it extended well beyond anyone person.

Southeast Christian Church in Louisville, Ky., is one of the largest congregations in North America. Though Senior Minister Bob Russell refuses to take any personal credit for the phenomenal growth of Southeast, one cannot help but see his influence. God has used him in many ways, but "speaking the truth in love" is certainly an example set by Russell for more than 30 years.

Being familiar with this church I was fascinated when I learn that when the new building was being built members were permitted to go into the auditorium, class rooms and hallways and wrote their favorite Bible verses. Today the whole structure has verses hidden by carpet, tile, floor covering and paint in every part of the building. It is said, many who remember where they wrote their verse often stop and thank God for His blessings.

Russell's influence has spread to the congregation. For

the past three decades, Southeast has been a moral and Christian lighthouse in the Louisville metropolitan area. The church has been the recipient of intense criticisms from liberal media and liberal religious groups for its positions on abortion, homosexuality, the exclusivity of salvation through Christ and other "hot-button issues." Despite the criticisms, the large congregation has maintained a spirit of love and grace. Many of the harshest critics express surprise at the gentle and loving spirit of the church when they visit.

Southeast Christian's ministries have made a profound impact on the Louisville community. The congregation knows that holding to truth with conviction is not mutually exclusive with being a people demonstrating Christ-like love.

In 160 of the 353 interviews conducted, slightly under half of the formerly unchurched described the churches they eventually joined as churches that were uncompromising in their convictions but Christ-like in their demeanor.

"I had this image of Baptists as mean-spirited and legalistic," Frank N. of Georgia told us. "But the church I connected with is anything but that. The church does have a clear doctrinal stand, but they are also one of the most loving groups of people I have ever been around."

Yes, doctrine really matters

Perhaps some people will be surprised to hear of the importance of doctrine in reaching the unchurched. The formerly unchurched, however, left little doubt of the importance of doctrine in their accepting Christ and choosing a church. They spoke with clarity of the issues that were important to them.

More formerly unchurched spoke of the importance of doctrine in their decision-making process than any other factor.

The doctrine that attracted the formerly unchurched was not just any belief system, but a theology that could best be described as conservative, evangelical and uncompromising.

Many indicated that their interest in doctrine was a consequence of their desire to discover absolutes in a culture where few absolutes are perceived to exist.

Those who spoke of the importance of doctrine could discern easily where churches were strong or weak in their affirmation of beliefs. The formerly unchurched were attracted to churches that had doctrinal certitude.

The pastor was the key person to whom the formerly unchurched looked for certitude of beliefs. They did not look to the pastor alone, however, but to the entire congregation.

It appears that doctrinal conviction not only attracts the unchurched, but it may have a major role in their assimilation after they become Christians.

The evidence is clear, if not overwhelming: doctrine really matters. Church leaders will ignore this reality to their church's peril. The insights of the formerly unchurched have been intriguing and helpful. An entire set of strategies could be developed from the information we gleaned from them. But unless church leaders are willing, even eager, to do what is necessary to reach the unchurched, the information is of little value. In other words, leadership is critical.

God fully expected the church of Jesus Christ to prove itself as a miraculous body in the midst of a hostile world.

Christians should be in contact with the world but in being and spirit separated from it—and as such, they should be the most amazing people in the world.

In an article I did for *Contact Magazine, Nashville, Tennessee,* I addressed the problem we would have with doctrine in our churches in **The People the Twenty-first Century Church has**

forgotten.

I'm afraid the church in the future will be a reflection of its past. The same problems it will have in the future came because of its negligence to do what it should have done in the decades before. If the church was ever really active to God's expectation, then the church in now in remission. God fully expected the church of Jesus Christ to prove itself as a miraculous body in the midst of a hostile world. Christians should be in contact with the world but in being and spirit separated from it—and as such, they should be the most amazing people in the world.

18

Organize! Organize! Organize!
Do you have a Vision Statement?

Start with a Vision Statement.
VISION STATEMENT
And Jesus came and spoke to them, saying, "All authority has been given to Me in heaven and on earth. Go therefore and make disciples of all the nations, baptizing them in the name of the Father and of the Son and of the Holy Spirit, teaching them to observe all things that I have commanded you; and I am with you always, even to the end of the age." Amen. (Matthew 28:18-20)
To help lead my local church to fulfill the Great Commission by:

     1.   Evangelizing the lost
     2.   Discipling the saved

Every organization, no matter what it is, must have a vision which gives it purpose and focus. The vision which you establish gives the much needed direction for the work of the organization. What are the purpose and the mission of the Sunday school? The priority of the Sunday school is to lead the church to become a New Testament church by fulfilling the twofold mission of the

Great Commission. Sunday school is the foundational strategy in a local church for building Great Commission Christians through Bible study groups that engage people in evangelism, discipleship, fellowship, ministry and worship. The Sunday school is the only organization in the local body with the specific task of reaching people; therefore, it is critical that our main objective should be reaching the lost and unchurched. If the Sunday school does not reach the lost and unchurched people then the Sunday school and ultimately every other organization in the Church will regress. If the Sunday school does not reach people, then the whole Church will suffer.

Then establish a strategy.
SUNDAY SCHOOL VISION STRATEGY
I. Develop New Leaders
2. Birth New Units
3. Evangelism

The Sunday school Vision Strategy answers the question how. Once we have a vision statement that establishes our purpose and our mission then we must have a strategy in order to make this vision a reality. The strategy is a step by step process to be sure we achieve our goal.

First Step
The key to reaching new people is new units. If the key to reaching new people is new units, then the key to birthing new units is new leaders. The Sunday school must always be in the process of developing new leadership within each class. In order for a new unit to survive two elements must be present; a genuine need and genuine leadership. However, new units based on need alone will eventually fizzle out and die. For a new unit to succeed strong leadership must be coupled with and precede the need.

Second Step

For the Sunday school to be able to continually reach the lost and to continually be able to minister to all the needs of the church, it must continually birth new units. New units are the only way to facilitate new people! New units will certainly grow faster than old ones, and new units mean new people, which mean new growth.

Third Step

One of the largest parts of Sunday school should be to train workers in evangelism. If the church is to carry out the Great Commission then the Sunday school needs to train its members how to be soul winners. The program best suited to help the Sunday school achieve this goal is an evangelism strategy specifically for the Sunday school... It helps the Sunday school to be what it is intended to be; the foundational strategy in a local church for leading people to faith in the Lord Jesus Christ and for building Great Commission Christians through Bible study groups that engage people in evangelism, discipleship, fellowship, ministry and worship.

Bible Study *is the foundational strategy in a local church for leading people to faith in the Lord Jesus Christ and for building Great Commission Christians through open Bible study groups that engage people in evangelism, discipleship, ministry, fellowship, and worship.*

In other words, Sunday school is a strategy that guides people to come to know Jesus and then begin to deepen their lives in evangelism, discipleship, ministry, fellowship, and worship. The goal of the teaching that takes place during the Sunday school hour is to lead people to encounter the life-changing experience of knowing Jesus and learning what it means to follow Him! The Sunday school is an open group because it serves as an entry point into the church for unbelievers. An open group is primarily an evangelistic Bible study group or event comprised of unbelievers and believers. Bible study groups that are designed primarily to reach lost people are open groups and Bible study groups that are designed primarily for moving saved people toward spiritual maturity are closed groups. Sunday school as an open group is recommended as the best proven organizational framework for involving families and individuals in the evangelistic work of the church.

One of the most important person you will want for leadership is the Superintendent. This person will be the leader if the Sunday school is going to grow. Below is a guideline for selecting this individual.

THE SUNDAY SCHOOL SUPERINTENDENT

The office of the Sunday school Superintendent carries with it great responsibility. It should also carry with it corresponding authority. However, it is authority that goes with leadership rather than that of management.

The superintendent is appointed and put in charge of the church's Sunday school. The success of the school is thereby entrusted to him. If the Sunday school is a success, it is because he makes it so. If it is a failure, he cannot shift the responsibility for failure upon the shoulders of others. He alone is responsible.

I. Requirements

A. Definition:
The Sunday school Superintendent is the educational executive who is in charge of the Sunday school system: its officers, teachers, and pupils.

He should be superintendent of the Sunday school with all that word Superintendent means. According to Webster the word superintendent means, "One who has the oversight and

charge of some place, institution, department, or the like."
  B.   Qualifications
       1.   He must be a Christian.
       2.   He must be a church member.
       3.   He must be consecrated.
       4.   He must be cooperative.
       5.   He must be congenial.
       6.   He must be comprehensive
            ▪   He must know his own school: equipment, curriculum, records, and personnel.
            ▪   He must understand the thrust of his churches program.
            ▪   He must ever be willing to broaden his knowledge of Sunday school methods.
       7.   He must be a commander.
            a.   He should be aggressive but not domineering.
            b.   He should be progressive but not oppressive.
            c.   He must be persevering.
            d.   He must be visionary.
  C.   Relationships
       1.   To the pastor
            a.   The pastor and superintendent should have a common interest.
            b.   The pastor and superintendent should be in accord.
            c.   The pastor provides the dynamics and the superintendent directs the mechanics.
       2.   To the Board of Christian Education
Since this board has the responsibility of directing the total educational program of the church, and since the

superintendent serves on it as the representative of the Sunday school, it is his task to act as liaison between the board and the staff of the Sunday school.

3. to the Sunday school Staff

The superintendent will work with the departmental superintendents who implement the program with the teachers and pupils in their departments.

II. Regulate Total Organization

      A. Adopt a Sunday school Standard.

      A standard provides a set of goals for the Sunday school.

      B. Advocate sound organizational structure.

      Departmentalize and grade by ages as the ideal.

      C. Administer a balanced program.

      Instruction, worship, service, and social activities.

III. Retain Good Personnel

      A. Supply tasks which are related to abilities.

      In addition to the general superintendent, the staff needed includes a general secretary and treasurer; leadership for departments including a superintendent, secretary, pianist, teachers, required to operate a Sunday school, but there are additional opportunities for service.

      B. Stimulate growth through teacher-training.

      1. Perennial Elective Sunday school class, Training Hour, preceding prayer meeting, regular worker's conference.

      2. Annual Two week course, annual denominational conference, interdenominational conventions, or week-end retreats.

      C. Show appreciation

      Express appreciation to the Sunday school staff by workers banquets, letters, or certificates, convention trips.

IV. **Recruits New Staff Members**

    A.   Pray for leaders needed. Luke 10:2

    B.   Prepare a talent survey.

        Use a questionnaire to determine the abilities and interest of the church constituency.

        Also check Vacation Bible School and Camp Staff to be sure that these people have an area of service throughout the year.

    C.   Proceed with an enlistment day service.

        This is a time when a spiritual challenge is given by the pastor followed by an invitation to dedication for further Christian service. Those responding then enter into training and finally into service.

    D.   Protect program against inefficient personnel.

- Appointments are made by Board of Christian Education, not by an individual.
- An appointment should only last a year.
- The statement of standards of the Sunday school should help to highlight areas of inefficiency.
- The Board of Christian Education constantly studies personnel in relation to the program and seeks to overcome areas of weakness.

V.   **Renew through the Worker's Meeting.**

    A.   Initiate with fellowship.

        A dinner can be used to encourage prompt attendance and to contribute to a spirit of comradeship.

    B.   Inspire by worship.

        A spiritual challenge should be given at the beginning of each session.

C. Inform with facts.
- Each committee should report in writing.
- Plans for visitation can be made and prospects assigned.

D. Involve in departmental groups.

Problems which concern individual departments should be discussed at this time.

E. Interest with year's program for Sunday school.
- Determine the needs of the Sunday school staff and base objectives on these.
- List topics which would satisfy these objectives.
- Secure leaders who are competent to speak on these topics.
-

VI. Require Good Programs at the Sunday school Hour.

A. Set up standards for worship programs.

It is necessary that they be well planned.

B. Supervise each worship program.

Superintendent will be in Sunday school at least one half hour early each week to be sure that needed equipment is ready, the staff and pupils are greeted, and newcomers are made to feel welcome in their classes.

C. Stress special days.

These should be limited and well planned.

VII. Reach the Community

A. Publicize the church.

Newspaper publicity, printed bulletins, letters, radio, posters, etc. In some Sunday schools the superintendent appoints one individual who is in charge of promotion.

B.   Plan for visitation.
- 1st obligation is to those enrolled.
- 2nd obligation is to the un-churched in the families represented.
- 3rd obligation is to the un-churched in the immediate vicinity of the church.
- Sunday schools that plan definite times for visitation seem to secure better results.
- The visitors include officers, teachers, and pupils.
- The callers meet at the church for instruction and prayer, then the calling is done. They return to report their results.

VIII.   Record Results
A.   Establish sound record system.
- A committee should study various record systems and select the one which fits the needs.
- Statistics are important for they tell an important part of the story of the Sunday school.

B.   Enroll new members.
- Give a tentative class assignment until the departmental superintendent visits the home to determine the class suited to him.
- If transferring from another school, seek to secure a letter of transfer.
- Aim to involve the whole family in the program of the Sunday school.
- Keep accurate permanent records on the pupil's attendance and

    spiritual development.
- When the pupil is saved, encourage attendance in a church membership class.
- Seek to guide pupil into activities in the total church program.

CONCLUSION:

    From this study we learn that one man holds the key to the successful Sunday school. That man is the Sunday school Superintendent. The Sunday school cannot grow beyond the scope of his vision. He is God's man. "God's man in God's place gets God's work done."

Guidelines For Sunday school Teachers

    The teacher is one of the most important factors in the success, growth, and development of a Sunday school class. The class is made up of individuals within a specified age range, and possibly grouped by sex.

    The teacher will be a born-again believer in Jesus Christ, an active member of Heritage Church, and hold to Biblical inerrancy and other doctrines taught by Heritage Church.

    The specific responsibilities of the teacher are as follows:

    Attend. It is hope the teacher is able to attend Sunday morning worship, Sunday evening worship, Wednesday night worship, and visitation. By so doing, the teacher can be an example of faithfulness, and thus encourage faithfulness among class members. Teachers should avoid excessive planned absences (more than 2-4 Sundays per year). The teacher should notify his/her department director as far in advance of planned absences as possible. In the case of sudden, unexpected absences, the teacher should notify the assistant teacher or director as soon as practical.

Teach. The teacher will make every effort to effectively teach the specified Bible lesson to his/her pupils, under the leadership of God's Holy Spirit. The teacher will teach from the open Bible, rather than from a quarterly. Quarterlies, commentaries, and other resources should be used for study and preparation. The teacher's goal is to use a variety of teaching methods to lead the class members to discover the truths contained in the Bible passage, and to apply those truths to their everyday lives. Teachers are to strive for very practical application of Bible truths, so the members can live the lesson throughout their daily activities.

Organize. The teacher will see that his/her class is properly organized for outreach and ministry. The teacher will enlist all other class officers (outreach leader, care group leaders, activities leader, and secretary), and with their help organize the class into groups for ministry, encouragement and outreach purposes. The duties of class officers are:

The **outreach leader** is to encourage the class to be involved in reaching out to lost and unchurched persons within its specified age range, and to be certain the care group leaders are doing their jobs.

The **care group leader** is to contact every member of his group every week, build a relationship with each group member, minister to the group member, and encourage each group member to be faithful in attendance.

The **activities leader** is to plan and carry out fellowship activities for the class. Every fellowship activity should be used as an outreach opportunity, by inviting prospects to attend. The activities leader and teacher will work with their counterparts from other classes in planning and carrying out department-wide fellowship activities.

The **secretary** is to accurately record class attendance and contacts each week. The outreach leader may perform this function.

In Preschool and Children's classes there are multiple teachers, with one teacher being the lead teacher. In those classes, the teachers share the duties carried out by adult class officers.

Minister. The teacher will attempt to get to know the members within his class, and ask the Lord to help him teach the Bible to address those needs wherever possible. The teacher should visit in the home of each class member at least once a year, and minister to class members when alerted to specific needs by class officers.

Direct. The teacher will lead and direct the work of the class. The work of the class can be summarized as reaching people for Bible study, teaching the Bible, seeking to win persons to Christ, and developing (or maturing) Christians. The teacher will see that the other class officers are doing their jobs properly and faithfully (see class officer duties listed in number 3 above).

Encourage. The teacher will challenge and encourage each class officer and class member to become personally involved in the class' work of reaching, teaching, winning, and developing. As a part of this task, the teacher will be expected to take part in outreach visitation, and encourage each class officer and member to do the same.

Fellowship. Since fellowship and friendships are so needed in our modern, fast-paced world, the teacher will direct the activities leader to plan class fellowship activities on at least a quarterly basis. Fellowship activities should always be used as opportunities to reach out to prospects, as well as encourage members.

Plan. The teacher will make planning and preparation for teaching an important priority in his weekly schedule.

Guidelines For Care Group Leaders

The primary task of the care group leader in a youth or adult class is to minister to the members of his group by maintaining regular contact with them. The group will be made up of 4 - 7 class members assigned to the care, ministry, and leadership of a care group leader.

The care group leader will be a born again believer in Jesus Christ, and an active member of the Sunday school class. The care group leader should be regular in attendance and willing to be submissive to the leadership of his outreach leader and teacher.

The specific responsibilities of the care group leader are as follows:

Minister. The care group leader is to minister to the persons in his   group. As such, the care group leader serves as the primary minister to those persons. The care group leader should follow these guidelines:

Visit in the home of each group member. Find out all you can about the group member. Ask him to share his personal testimony, and share yours with him. Ask about needs in the person's life. Ask how you can pray for him.

Pray daily for your group members. Bring their needs to God and ask God to give you a heart full of love for that person.

Contact every group member every week. Through either a visit, phone call, or card, communicate with your group members weekly. Thank them for their attendance, or encourage them to come. Tell them you are praying for them. Love them where they hurt.

Vary your method of contact. Do not call every week, do not send a card every week, and do not visit every week. Use variety in your method and your message.

Tell your group members about special events such as revivals, guest preachers, or high attendance emphases

Communicate. Call your outreach leader every Saturday, and tell him about your contacts with you group members that week. Tell him how many group members you expect in attendance on Sunday. Also, tell your teacher or outreach leader about crises or special needs in your group members' lives.

Attend.   Attend class social functions and any planning meetings your teacher or outreach leader may have. Also, attend training events offered for care group leaders.

Guidelines For Outreach Leaders

The class outreach leader's primary task is to lead the class to reach out to lost and un-churched persons in their community. Each Sunday school class is responsible for reaching all prospects within that class' specified age range.

The outreach leader will be a born again believer in Jesus Christ, and an active member of Heritage Free Will Baptist Church. The outreach leader should be regular in attendance and willing to be submissive to the leadership of his teacher, department director, and church staff.

The specific responsibilities of the outreach leader are as follows:

Outreach. The outreach leader should keep outreach (lovingly reaching out to the unsaved and un-churched persons with the gospel message) constantly before the class. It is the outreach leader's job to encourage the class members to become actively involved in outreach. The outreach leader will do this through personal example (participating in visitation), verbal invitations, and constant encouragement.

On Sundays, the outreach leader should assign prospects to the members, so the members can visit, call, or write the prospects during the week. The outreach leader will also encourage class members to report their contacts each Sunday. A contact is any time an individual (member or prospect) is invited to Sunday school.

Organize. The outreach leader will help the teacher organize the class into groups for ministry and encouragement. The entire class shall be organized into groups of 4 - 7 members, and each group shall be under the care of a care group leader. The care group leader, then, is the primary minister to those 4 - 7 members. As new members join the class, the outreach leader will immediately assign them to a group. As the class grows, the teacher and outreach leader may need to enlist additional group leaders, and reorganize the groups.

Minister. The outreach leader fulfills the function of a care group leader in relation to the care group leaders. As such, the outreach leader will minister to the needs of the care group leaders. Also, he will be available to minister to other class members when called upon to do so.

Administer. The outreach leader serves as the teacher's assistant in the functioning of the class. As such, he will be available to help the teacher in any way the teacher may require. The outreach leader also oversees the work of the care group leaders, making sure that they do their jobs effectively.

Call. The outreach leader is to call each care group leader on Saturday, to make sure the care group leaders have contacted their group members. The outreach leader should then call the teacher to report on contacts made to class members, ministry needs, and anticipated attendance for Sunday.

Guidelines for Substitute Teachers

1.   When called upon to teach: pray, study, and prepare to present a life-changing, learner-involving Bible lesson each Sunday, based upon the curriculum supplied to you by Heritage Free Will Baptist Church.

2.   When called upon to teach: gather teaching materials, resources, and make copies needed for class before Sunday morning.

3.   When called upon to teach, carry out the "Sunday Duties" described above under the "Duties of Teachers."

Guidelines for Outreach Leaders (Adult Classes)

Attend Sunday school faithfully.

Participate in outreach and ministry visitation each week.

Encourage as many class members as possible to become involved in outreach and ministry visitation.

Manage the class prospect notebook. Keep it up to date.

Form visitation teams from within the class.

Assign prospects to the visitation teams.

Keep outreach before the class on a regular basis.

Lead the "Outreach Minute" each Sunday morning.

Invite and encourage people to participate in outreach and ministry visitation.

Tell how many prospects the class currently has.

Offer to pair up any without partners.

Encourage class members who visit at alternate times during the week to complete and turn in an "I Went Visiting" card.

Guidelines for Care Group Leaders (Adult Classes)

1.   Attend Sunday school faithfully.

2.   Contact each member in your group every week.

3.   Try to build a friendly relationship with each group member.

4.   Encourage your group members to attend Sunday school.

5.   Complete a "Care Group Leader Report" each week and turn it in to the Class Teacher on Sunday morning.

6.   Notify the Teacher of serious needs in the lives of care group members.

Guidelines for Class Greeters

Attend Sunday school faithfully.

9:00 - 9:15 a.m.:

1. Welcome members and visitors as they arrive.

2. Get complete info on all visitors.

3. Give the white copy of the enrollment/visitor slip to the

Class Secretary.
4. Give the yellow copy to the Class Coordinator.
5. Give the pink copy to the Outreach Leader.
6. Invite new people to enroll in Sunday school.
7. Introduce visitors to other class members and see that they are seated with members who will be friendly to them.
8. At the end of class:
9. Thank visitors for coming.
10. Offer to help those with young children locate the nursery.
11. Escort visitors to the Worship Center.
12. Be sure visitors are seated with class members in the worship service. If no one else sits with them the greeter should sit with them.
13. Assist ushers in getting visitor information to the visitors.
14. Encourage visitors to fill out the worship service visitor card.
15. At the conclusion of the service escort visitors to meet the Pastor.
16. See that their visitor card is dropped in an offering receptacle or handed to an usher.
17. Thank visitors for attending and offer to help them find their way to the nursery or to their vehicle, as needed.

Guidelines for Class Secretaries (Adult Classes)
1. Attend Sunday school faithfully.
2. Receive the class roll sheet and the prayer sheet after it has made its way around the room.
3. Check the roll sheet for errors.
4. Take a "head count" of the attendance and compare it to the attendance on the roll sheet. Make corrections as necessary.
5. Attach any enrollment/visitor forms to the roll

sheet.   Make sure the class number is written on every form.

6.   Attach any completed "I Went Visiting" cards to the roll sheet.

7.   Remove the prayer sheet from its clipboard.   Put the clipboard in the class basket

8.   Put the completed roll sheet in the class basket and place it outside the classroom door no later than 10:00 a.m.

9.   At 10:15 a.m. give the prayer sheet to the Class Teacher

Guidelines for Class Treasurers (Adult Classes)

1.   Attend Sunday school faithfully.

2.   Receive money that is collected from the class members.

3.   Safeguard such money and give a regular accounting of it to the Class Coordinator.

4.   Under the direction of the Class Coordinator use class money to meet special ministry needs in the lives of the class members.   Such ministry needs may include:

5.   Sending flowers, placing memorial Gideon Bibles, or making a gift to the church building fund in the event of the death of a member of a class member's family.

6.   Purchasing some of the food when taking a meal to a class member who is bereaved, sick, or has had a new baby.

18

Summary

During my years of Sunday school teaching of Teachers, I always kept an assortment of Stories that related to this organization I especially liked those whose testimony always recommend the importance of it in their lives.

One well-known man, the founder of Chick-Fil-A. S. Truett Cathy was also a great Sunday school Teacher and whose stores close on Sundays. He said, "I can't be teaching kids how to keep the Lord's Day holy while my cash registers are ringing."

Even in the most unusual times the Sunday share serious lessons like the one below.

The boy didn't speak. He came to Sunday school every week with his sister and sat on the woman's lap, but he never made a sound. Each week she would tell him all the way to Sunday school and all the way home, "I love you and Jesus loves you."

One day, to her amazement, the little boy turned around and stammered, "I—I love you, too." Then he put his arms around her and gave her a big hug.

That was 2:30 on a Saturday afternoon. At 6:30 that night, the boy was found dead in a garbage bag under a fire escape. His mother had beaten him to death and thrown his body in the trash.

"I love you and Jesus loves you." Those were some of the last words he heard in his short life—from the lips of a Puerto Rican woman who could barely speak English.

Who among us is qualified to minister? Who among us even knows what to do? Not you; not me. But I ran to an altar once, and I got some fire and just went. So did this woman who couldn't speak English. And so can you.

Some of the funniest stories comes from Sunday school. Such was the case of a third-grade Sunday school teacher who was uneasy about the lesson "Thou shalt not commit adultery." By way of introduction she asked, "Would someone please explain what adultery means? "A young lad answered matter-of-factly,"Adultery is when a kid lies about his age. "

Some years back as an adult Sunday school teacher, I'm was often given fact sheets on new members so I could invite them to visit our class. While reading about one new member, I chuckled when I read under the "Circumstances of Salvation" this notation: "Accepted Christ in high school. Was baptized but would like to be reimbursed [crossed out] immersed."

I am a believer in the value of Sunday school.

A minister tells the following, "When I was at Buckingham Palace last year, Prince Philip asked me, "What can we do about crime here in England?"
I replied, "Send more children to Sunday school." He thought I was joking. But I pointed out a study by sociologist Christie Davies, which found that in the first half of the 1800s British society was marked by high levels of crime and violence, which

dropped dramatically in the late 1800s and early 1900s. What changed an entire nation's national character? Throughout that period, attendance at Sunday schools rose steadily until, by 1888, a full 75 percent of children in England were enrolled. Since then, attendance has fallen off to one-third its peak level, with a corresponding increase in crime and disorder. If we fill the Sunday schools, we can change hearts and restore society.

While Sunday school has its days of sincerity and also fills the minds of the unknowing with the humor that flows from it. It is truly astonishing what happens in Bible stories when they are retold by young scholars around the world. Such is the following.

God got tired of creating the world, so he took the Sabbath off. Adam and Eve were created from an apple tree. Noah's wife was called Joan of Ark. Lot's wife was a pillar of salt by day, but a ball of fire by night.

Samson was a strongman who let himself be led astray by a Jezebel like Delilah. Samson slayed the Philistines with the axe of the apostles.

Moses led the Hebrews to the Red Sea, where they made unleavened bread made without any ingredients. The Egyptians were all drowned in the desert. Afterward, Moses went up on Mount Cyanide to get the Ten Amendments.

The First Commandment was when Eve told Adam to eat the apple. The Fifth Commandment is to humor thy father and mother. The Seventh Commandment is thou shalt not admit adultery.

Moses died before he ever reached Canada. Then Joshua led the Hebrews in the Battle of Geritol. The greatest miracle in the Bible is when Joshua told his son to stand still and he obeyed him.

David was a Hebrew king skilled at playing the liar. He fought with the Finklesteins, a race of people who lived in biblical times. Solomon, one of David's sons, had three hundred wives and seven hundred porcupines.

Jesus enunciated the Golden Rule, which says to do one to others before they do one to you. The people who followed the Lord were called the Twelve Decibels. The epistles were the wives of the apostles. One of the opossums was St. Matthew who was by profession a taxi man.

St. Paul cavorted to Christianity. He preached holy acrimony, which is another name for marriage. A Christian should have only one wife. This is called monotony.

Another funny thing from my files was the lesson about an irate father who phoned the Sunday school superintendent after his daughter had been attending a few weeks. "Our preschooler tells me if she misses Sunday school too often, you'll pitch her into the furnace! What in the world are you teaching in that church?"

Investigating the matter, the superintendent questioned the teacher. At first stumped, they finally put two and two together: Stressing the importance of regular attendance on Sundays, the teacher had told her class that if they missed four consecutive weeks, they would be dropped from the register.

Now to a serious note about one of my heroes who started hundreds of Sunday schools and churches as a young man. I will let D. L. Moody tell his own story.

When I first began to work for God in Chicago, a Boston business man was converted there and stayed three months, and when leaving he said to me that there was a man living on such a street in whom he was very much interested, and whose boy was in the high school, and he had said that he had two brothers and a little sister who didn't go anywhere to Sabbath school, because their parents would not let them. This gentleman said to me—

"I wish you would go round and see them."

I went, and I found that the parents lived in a drinking saloon, and that the father kept the bar. I stepped up to him and told him what I wanted, and he said he would rather have his sons become drunkards and his daughter a harlot, than have them go to our schools. It looked pretty dark, and he was very harsh to me; but I went a second time, thinking that I might catch him in a better humor. He ordered me out again. I went a third time and found him in a better humor. He said—

"You are talking too much about the Bible. I will tell you what I will do; if you teach them something reasonable, like Paine's *Age of Reason,* they may go."

Then I talked further to him, and finally he said, "If you will read Paine's book, I will read the New Testament."

Well, to get hold of him I promised, and he got the best of the bargain. We exchanged books, and that gave me a chance to call again and talk with that family.

One day he said, "Young man, you have talked so much about church, now you can have a church down here."

"What do you mean?"

"Why, I will invite some friends, and you can come down here and preach to them; not that I believe a word you say, but I do it to see if it will do fellows like us any good."

"Very well," I said; "now let us have it distinctly understood that we are to have a certain definite time."

He told me to come at eleven o'clock, saying, "I want you to understand that you are not to do all the preaching."

"How is that?"

"I shall want to say something, and also my friends."

I said, "Supposing we have it understood that you are to have forty-five minutes and I fifteen; is that fair?"

He thought that was fair. He was to have the first forty-five, and I the last fifteen minutes. I went down, and the saloon-keeper wasn't there. I thought perhaps he had backed out; but I found the reason was that he had found that his saloon was not large enough to hold all his friends, and he had gone to a neighbor's, whither I went and found two rooms filled. There were atheists, infidels, and scoffers there. I had taken a little boy with me, thinking he might aid me. The moment I got in they plied me with all sorts of questions.

But I said I hadn't come to hold any discussion; that they had been discussing for years and had reached no conclusion. They took up the forty-five minutes of time talking, and the result was there were no two who could agree.

Then came my turn. I said, "We always open our meetings with prayer; let us pray." I prayed, and said perhaps someone else would pray before I got through. After I finished, the little boy prayed. I wish you could have heard him. He prayed to God to have mercy upon those men who were talking so against His beloved Son. His voice sounded more like an angel's than a human voice. After we got up, I was going to speak, but there was not a dry eye in the assembly. One after another went out, and the old man I had been after for months—and sometimes it looked pretty dark—came and, putting his hand on my shoulder with tears streaming down his face, said—"Mr. Moody, you can have my children go to your Sunday school."

The next Sunday they came, and after a few months the oldest boy, a promising young man then in the high school, came upon the platform; and with his chin quivering and the tears in his eyes said, "I wish to ask these people to pray for me; I want to become a Christian."

God heard and answered our prayers for him. Amongst all my acquaintances I don't know of a man whom it seemed more hopeless to reach. I believe if we lay ourselves out for the work, there is not a man but can be reached and saved. I don't care who he is, if we go in the name of our Master, and persevere, it will not be long before Christ will bless us, no matter how hard their heart is. "We shall reap, if we faint not."

35 Years of Workshop
Notes and Helps

LEADERSHIP | CHARACTER

Dr. Alton Loveless

The above book is available from Amazon for $6.95 in an 8 ½ x 11 format with 138 pages suitable for photocopying to use in your own training program.

I spent 35 years active in Teacher Training workshops, Christian Education and Interpersonal Relationship seminars in this country and abroad presenting more than 1100. I traveled, spoke, was used as a consultant, or conducted seminars in 69 denominations and independent churches in all 50 of the States with the exception of Nebraska and North Dakota. I performed various roles in all the provinces of Canada, but five, and in 38 other foreign countries. The notes in this book represents some of those workshop programs.

*9 7 8 1 9 4 0 6 0 9 2 1 8 *